FAMILY ITALY

FAMILY ITALY

FRANK BARRETT

BOXTREE

First published in Great Britain in 1994 by Boxtree Limited

10 9 8 7 6 5 4 3 2 1

Printed in Finland, by WSOY

Boxtree Limited
Broadwall House
21 Broadwall
London SE1 9PL

A CIP catalogue entry for this book is available from the British Library

ISBN 1 85283 541 9

Designed by Blackjacks, London

Cover design by Robert Updegraff

Front cover photograph courtesy of Tony Stone Images

CONTENTS

FOREWORD

Over the past 12 months, since I began researching this book, I have to admit that I have suffered a crisis of faith. Having been a committed Francophile for as long as I can remember, I have now fallen deeply and madly in love with Italy.

Don't get me wrong, I'm still very keen on France (we're still on speaking terms), it's just that I suddenly feel very passionate about the pleasures of Italy. It started with a weekend trip in November to Venice. Everybody said November would be a terrible month to see Venice: cold, bleak and unattractive. It was certainly cold (it snowed) – but bleak and unattractive? They couldn't have been more wrong.

The city was wonderful – the fact that it was out of season added simply to its attraction. Empty alleyways, uncrowded piazzas, no cars, the smell of bread baking, the sounds of a fruit market, a mid-morning *cappuccino* in a crowded bar, a vaporetto trip down the Grand Canal. Certainly the canals and the grand buildings of Venice are uniquely gorgeous, but for me the real charm of the city is that in many ways it offers the best of the essence of Italy.

Suddenly, I'm addicted. I can't stop going back. It's not difficult to see why. For a family holiday, the country is perfect. Food like pasta and pizza which all children like, good sightseeing, relaxed family seaside resorts, an excellent choice of good value self-catering places (many with their own swimming pools) and people who enjoy having children around.

In producing this book I am grateful to all the tour operators who generously took the time to provide information about their holidays. As always I am also indebted to Sheila Barrett who did most of the hard work.

I hope this book encourages you to fall in love with Italy for yourself. If you are travelling to Italy for your first holiday, you should beware – the country is habit-forming.

Frank Barrett, April 1994

INTRODUCTION

Imagine being sat down with a piece of blank paper, and told to design the perfect country for family holidays. When your task is complete I'm pretty certain you will have ended up with something that looks very much like Italy. Most countries claim to have something for everybody. Few however can match Italy's extensive range of attractions and delights. The country really does have just about everything for the perfect family holiday.

If it were nothing more than good beaches and stunning countryside you were after, Italy has ample supplies of both. From smart beach resorts on the Adriatic Riviera to quiet villages in the gentle tree-lined Tuscan hills, or from the craggy Dolomites to the sleepy Sicilian shores, Italy's range of scenery is hard to beat .

But there is more – much more. A sublime Lake district – with the gorgeous Lakes Como, Garda, Maggiore and Orta it is perhaps the greatest of all Lake Districts; glorious mountain ranges with good walking, challenging biking and fine skiing and, of course, the finest historic cities in the world. Rome and Florence would be more than sufficient history and ancient elegance for most countries; but not for Italy which in addition can boast five-star places like Verona, Siena, Milan, Naples – and arguably the most wonderful of all cities: Venice.

For families, Italy is a particularly good destination because children are genuinely welcomed everywhere – even in the smartest hotels and restaurants. In family-run restaurants, for example, do not be surprised if waitresses gather up your children to take them off to the kitchens to ply them with sweet-meats. And, of course, if it's good food you want, then Italy takes the palm in this too. (Italians will be happy to tell you that it was they who taught the art of cooking to the French!) For families the Italian diet of pizza and pasta is perfect (what child will refuse a slice of pizza followed by a bowl of sumptuous Italian ice-cream?) – and of course thanks to the ailing state of the lire (even more ailing than the British pound) it is excellent value too.

I first visited Italy on a short cross-border day's outing in the early Sixties during a family camping holiday in the South of France. As natives of the Welsh valleys, we were surprised to discover that in some ways Italy was a much less foreign place to us than France. In the first half of this century, South Wales attracted many thousands of Italian immigrants most of whom seem to have opened up a cafe or restaurant (it was this same wave of emigration that brought Charles Forte to Scotland). While the only French person you were likely to meet in Wales was the once-a-year onion seller – the Johnny Onion man who travelled on a push-bike garlanded in strings of onions – Italians were a well regarded feature of the community. Thanks to their influence we knew all about Italian ice cream and frothy coffee – I don't think we knew it then as *cappuccino* – and later we began to learn about the delights of pizza and spaghetti.

When we crossed the border on that day-trip back then in the early Sixties, it was obvious to even my childish eyes that Italy was quite a different proposition to France. The Italians were more excitable, their conversation was noticeably oper-atic, their driving was atrocious. While the French had an occa-sional tendency towards off-handedness and *hauteur* (a French word, you notice), the Italians were never less than warm and welcoming.

In 1966 I returned for a longer holiday with my aunt who took me to the resort of Lido di Jesolo on the Adriatic Riviera. Because of the problems of operating charter flights to Italy at that time, our Cosmos package involved a charter flight from the unlikely departure point of Manston in Kent (a Royal Air Force base, I seem to recall) to Basle in a rickety plane with propellers and a leaky roof. This flight was followed by a seemingly endless coach ride up and down switchback roads over the mountains and into Italy. (Do you remember the closing scene of the Michael Caine film *The Italian Job* which left a coach see-sawing terrifyingly over a precipice? Every sharp turn made by our coach conjured up just such a nightmare.)

For someone whose principal experience of seaside resorts was Barry Island and Weston-super-Mare, Lido di Jesolo was undoubtedly something of a revelation. It wasn't just that the sun was perpetually roasting hot or that the sea was azure blue and as warm as bath water, to my eyes Lido was stylish, elegant and – most impressive of all – it was alive. My full day excursion to Venice would have been the highlight of the trip if it hadn't been for the fact that on the following day England won the World Cup (a victory made all the sweeter by the fact that half of our hotel was occupied by Germans).

A visit to Italy is an education in the art of enjoying life: the Italian love of life, expressed in everything from paintings and architecture to eating and drinking, is a complete contrast to the wintry greyness of British life (by comparison to the Italians, much of British life is wintry grey even in summer!). It is easy to see why the country became the first significant foreign holiday destination for the British.

A man who has not been in Italy, wrote Dr Johnson, is always conscious of an inferiority. Since the 18th century when the early British Grand Tourists headed for Rome, Italy has always claimed a special place in our affections. Italy had many reasons for attracting early tourists: there were the glories of ancient Rome (as a place of Christian pilgrimage it was second only to Jerusalem) which along with Florence and Venice comprised three of the most important cities for European art and architecture. For 19th century aesthetes like Byron, Shelley and Keats, a visit to Italy was an indispensable part of their education.

With its mighty cultural and historical heritage Italy has always held a deep fascination for the sophisticated tourist. But when it comes to thinking about self-catering holidays in the countryside, nowadays we tend to consider only France and the gite. But Italy was in this business decades before France.

As far as tourism is concerned, France is a relative newcomer. French regions like the Dordogne and Gascony – now so popular with the British holidaymaker – were until 20 or 30 years ago almost completely unknown. They were back-waters – largely sad, neglected places populated by poverty-stricken peasant farmers. In those days tourists went to the French coast not to the countryside.

By contrast the British have been holidaying in Tuscany – in its cities and its countryside – for almost 300 years. True, it has often been a rarefied sort of tourism. Like most visitors travel-ling in search of cultural enrichment, Lucy Honeychurch, the

Edwardian heroine of E M Forster's novel *A Room with a View*, came on her Grand Tour to Tuscany to discover a vibrant country of colour, passion, art and excitement – a place so different from her staid Home Counties world. For Forster, Italy was not so much a country, more a state of mind – agreeably at odds with the stultefying Victorianism of England. *'One doesn't come to Italy for niceness,'* exclaims a character in the novel: *'one comes for life.'*

Amusingly, the Department of Trade and Industry antagonised the Italian Embassy in London at the end of 1993 by producing some notes on *do's* and *don'ts* for British businessmen trading in Italy. Among the controversial advice offered in the leaflet was the information that Italians are frivolous, loud and that they don't tell the truth! Confirming that the British still find it difficult to understand the Italian lust for life, the DTI sanctimoniously warned readers: *'Don't be surprised at the noise level in bars, restaurants and on public transport. By British standards, there is no such thing as private Italian conversations and nobody whispers; the cacophony at meetings can be off-putting and deafening to British ears.'* E M Forster would no doubt have been greatly amused at this wooden-headed explanation of Italian life.

While the British have never really ever left Tuscany since the days of *A Room with a View,* the pleasures of the countryside which surrounds Florence and Siena have so far been enjoyed by a rather select aristocratic group whose enthusiastic patronage has given the area the nickname of 'Chianti-shire'. (A society deliciously sent up in John Mortimer's comic novel *A Summer's Lease.*)

But as in most holiday innovations, the aristocratic and the well-heeled lead the way. At the turn of the Century, after the 'colonisation' of the cultural and historic sites of Italy, the early British upper-class tourists went on to establish themselves in the seaside towns, mainly on the Italian Riviera – particularly the stretch of coast between Genoa and the French border. Naples and resorts in the Neapolitan area like Sorrento, Positano and Amalfi – and, of course, the island of Capri – have also long enjoyed a loyal and understandably enthusiastic following. In more recent times, as I discovered in the Sixties, the thrust of development has been along the Adriatic coast, easily accessible by road from Germany, Switzerland and Austria.

According to Italian tourist office statistics, the most popular areas of Italy for tourism (in order of popularity) are the Veneto (the region including and surrounding Venice), Emilia Romagna (the area south of Veneto including Rimini and Bologna), Trentino-Alto Adige (immediately south of the Austrian border), Tuscany (including Florence, Siena and Pisa), Lombardy (Milan and the Italian Lakes) and Lazio (Rome and surrounding area).

Surprisingly, with the exception of the island of Sicily, tourism has barely touched the southernmost fringes of the country. Areas like Puglia and Calabria are practically virgin territory for holidaymakers.

TIME FOR GROWTH?

With all that it has to offer, it is strange that compared with France or Spain relatively few British visitors enjoy the holiday pleasures of Italy. Distance is certainly a factor. While the French Dordogne is a comfortable day's drive from Le Havre, Florence is a very long drive from the Channel – a minimum of 14 hours from Calais which for most people will probably mean two overnight stops. (Some may consider this a problem – others may see the drive as a pleasant extension to the holiday, offering a chance to visit interesting places en route.)

Flying is the most practical way of getting to Italy for a holiday; unlike France, which is best reached by car. Italy is therefore at something of a disadvantage. But Spain is just as far away as Italy, and people are apparently very happy to fly to Spain in great numbers. If geography is a significant impediment, it is not the principal obstacle. Italy's main disincentive for the British tourists has been price. Over the past 20 years Italy has moved up the league table of the most expensive European holiday destinations. In 1976, for example, on average the UK tourist spent £7 per day on holiday in Italy (by comparison travellers to France spent £7.60 per day). By 1991, however, a visitor to Italy was spending on average £34 per day, while the traveller in France was paying only £27.60 per day. Italy had become one of the most expensive holiday destinations – more expensive even than Switzerland – exceeded only by Sweden (£43.50 per day) and Austria (£39.10 per day).

The rising costs of a holiday in Italy over the past decade have had a drastic effect on tourism. In 1976 Italy welcomed

726,000 UK visitors; this had risen to 1.05m by 1981 – but since then the total has grown only modestly, standing at 1.15m in 1991. France however has seen its total of UK tourists grow from 2.14m in 1976 to over 7.3m in 1991. And it's not just the numbers of visitors that have been affected, their total length of stay in Italy has declined. In 1976 British visitors on average spent 14.4 days on holiday in Italy; by 1991 this had slipped to 11.6 days. The UK now ranks as the sixth biggest market for Italy, after Switzerland, Germany, France, Austria and the former Yugoslavia.

But now there are signs that this negative trend in tourism to Italy is slowly being reversed. Thanks to the plunging value of the Italian lire (which happily has managed to plunge further than the Pound), for the past year Italy has been a much more economically priced holiday destination.

Led by a revival in ski holiday bookings (the relative strength of their currencies has made France, Switzerland and Austria more expensive winter sports destinations than Italy), Italy believes it is turning a corner. And the fact that the country effectively missed out on the package holiday boom of the Seventies and Eighties is now proving to be in Italy's favour. During the Seventies and early Eighties while the Spanish costas, the Algarve and many Greek islands were happy to turn large swathes of beautiful coastline into very unbeautiful tower block hotel resorts, Italy resisted the trend.

Now, as people react against the concept of the traditional Costa holiday and demand something more sophisticated, Italy proves to be more and more in line with changing contemporary taste. Certainly the most significant trend of recent years is the increasing number of British people who have rapidly begun to rediscover the attractions that made Italy so popular with earlier generations. Now a new generation of holidaymakers is set to discover Tuscany and the rest of Italy. A generation of travellers brought up on the rural delights of France, familiar with the self-catering gite are venturing beyond the familiar fields of Provence and the Dordogne and discovering a new sort of holiday.

In France, there is excellent scenery, there are agreeable towns, fine cuisine, good wine – but in Italy, there is all of this and more: there is, as E M Forster wrote, *life*.

THE BEST OF ITALY

In this book, as in previous editions, I hope to alert you to the best of the holiday possibilities offered by Italy. To provide a taste of the best of the country has to offer, here is my selection of Italian superlatives – I would be pleased to hear your nominations (the best recommendations will earn a free edition of the revised *Family Italy*).

Best all-round Italian holiday company

The wide range of different programmes it offers – from weekend breaks to self-catering as well as its own excellent programme of cheap flights available under the Sky Shuttle brand – make the Granada-owned Air Travel Group the leader in the field. See page 18

Best Italian Self-catering Specialist

The luscious selection of self-catering brochures available from International Chapters provides hours of delightful reading as you ponder the competing charms of Tuscan country houses and Venetian palazzos. See page 147

Best Holiday Region

If Italy is the perfect country for a family holiday, then Tuscany is arguably the perfect region of a perfect country. Superb places for self-catering, outstanding hotels, fabulous scenery, stunning art treasures (Michelangelo's *David* and Botticelli's *Birth of Venus* in Florence, for example), breathtaking ancient monuments (the Leaning Tower of Pisa), and much, much more besides. See page 95

Best city break

You've heard all the clichés about Venice: the most romantic city in the world, a city for lovers, la *Serenissima* – all the clichés are true. Venice is the most beautiful, most charming, most elegant, most stylish, most mysterious, most wonderful city break place you can ever hope to visit. See page 120

Best seaside resort

Taormina may not be quite beside the sea – the main town sits high on a Sicilian hill overlooking not only the sea but with a breathtaking view of Mount Etna and its ever-present plume of volcanic smoke. This small geographic detail however should

not exclude Taormina from the title of best Italian seaside place: it has the best of everything – shops, restaurants, bars, hotels and a stunning Greek amphitheatre to boot.
See page 106

Best Italian treat
Where to start? The food, of course: pasta of every shape, texture and colour – and all of it thoroughly delicious; then there's pizza; and don't forget the ice-cream; and Baci chocolates. Other treats? Opera – you've never seen opera until you've seen it in Italy. Volcanoes. A boat ride in Venice. Walking by night in Rome. A football match.

THE WORST OF ITALY . . .

- Driving. Italians are possibly the worst drivers in the whole of Europe. Attempting to negotiate the streets of Rome for the first time is a genuine white knuckle-ride. Italians drive as if their life depends on it – and occasionally it does!

- Parking. Italians park as badly as they drive. There are rarely enough parking spaces, so Italians have to park in any way they can, riding up on to the pavement with little regard for pedestrians. In Florence you can spend hours circling around in search of an elusive parking space.

- Queuing. Waiting in line is not a concept familiar to the Italians. If they want to do something, they want to do it *now*. If you are prepared to let people push in ahead of you, then they are quite happy to do it. For anyone with fond feelings for fair play, the wait in line for the Uffizi Gallery in Florence is a maddening experience.

- Smoking. Cigarettes may be going out of style in Britain; in Italy however, the dangers of lung cancer seem less of a concern. Almost everybody seems to smoke – not much fun if everybody in the restaurant lights up at the same time.

- Cellular phones. Half of Italy appears to own a mobile phone and all of them seem to be out on the street using them. Picking your way through a street littered with people engaged in deep conversation can be a hazardous business.

I hope you enjoy *Family Italy*: if you have any comments, suggestions or recommendations, please write to me at PO Box 67, Bath.

If you are travelling to Italy for a holiday, may I wish you a very pleasant trip.

1

Planning a holiday

Your local high street travel agency will mainly be able to offer you information on two sorts of Italian holiday: beach holidays and city breaks. With agencies increasingly concentrating on the sun and sand packages of the major operators, Italy has suffered since most of the operators who feature it are small independents.

Even if you want a beach holiday or a city break, travel agencies will only be able to offer a small choice of the big selection of the programmes currently available. In this book we attempt to offer as complete a guide as possible to inclusive holidays to Italy

Finding Out Information

Tourist Office in the UK: The Italian State Tourist Office (ENIT), 1 Princes Street, London W1R 8AY (071-408 1254; fax 071-493 6695). Walk-in visitors can pick up a good range of leaflets and brochures and seek answers to questions. Seeking information by mail or by phone is possible but usually inefficient or time-consuming or both. For detailed answers to questions, direct them to the appropriate regional tourist office (see below).

Regional tourist offices

The international dialling code for Italy is 010 39 (omit the first zero from the local area code):

Abruzzo
Viale Bovio, 425
65100 Pescara
Tel: 085-7671
Fax: 085-71789

Aosta Valley
Piazza Narbonne 3
11100 Aosta
Tel: 0165-303725
Fax: 0165-40134

Apulia
Corso Italia, 15
70123 Bari
Tel: 080-401111
Fax: 080-404564

Basilicata
Via Anzio, 44
85100 Potenza
Tel: 0971-332406
Fax: 0971-332630

Calabria
Vico III Rafaelli
88100 Catanzaro
Tel: 0961 8511
Fax: 0961 63143

Campania
Via Santa Lucia, 81
80132 Napoli
Tel: 081-7961111
Fax: 0861-7962027

Emilia-Romagna
Via Aldo Moro, 38
40127 Bologna
Tel: 051-283111
Fax: 051-283380

Friuli-Venezia Julia
Via S Francesco d'Assisi, 37
34133 Trieste
Tel: 040-7355
Fax: 040-362109

Latium
Via R Raimondi Garibaldi, 7
00145 Roma
Tel: 06-54571
Fax: 06-5115053

Liguria
Via Fieschi, 15
16121 Genova
Tel: 010 54851
Fax: 010 590218

Lombardy
Via Fabio Fitzi, 22
20124 Milano
Tel: 02-67651
Fax: 02-67655403

The Marches
Via Gentile da Fabriano
60100 Ancona
Tel: 071-8061
Fax: 071-8062117

Molise
Via Mazzini, 94
86100 Campobasso
Tel: 0874-9491
Fax: 0874-949523

Piedmont
Via Magenta, 12
10128 Torino
Tel: 011-43211
Fax: 011-4322440

Sardinia
Viale Trento
09100 Cagliari
Tel: 070-6061
Fax: 070-6062579

Sicily
Via Emanuele Notarbartolo, 9
90141 Palermo
Tel: 091-6961111
Fax: 091-6968135

11

Autonomous Province of Trent
Corso 3 Novembre, 132
38100 Trento
Tel: 0461-89511
Fax: 0461-982435

Trentino/Alto Adige
Autonomous Province of
Bolzano: Via Raiffeisen, 5
39100 Bolzano
Tel: 0471-993666
Fax: 0471-993699

Tuscany
Via di Novoli, 26
50127 Firenze
Tel: 055-439311
Fax: 055-4383064

Umbria
Corso Vannucci, 30
06100 Perugia
Tel: 075-6961
Fax: 075-5042483

Venetia
Palazzo Balbi
Dorsoduro 3901
30123 Venezia
Tel: 041-792828
Fax: 041-792948

GUIDEBOOKS

Given Italy's popularity with the independent traveller, it should not be surprising that there is a wide range of guide books covering almost every aspect of the country.

The three best books covering the whole of Italy are *Italy: The Rough Guide* (Rough Guides, £12.99) and *Italy: Travel Survival Kit* (Lonely Planet, £11.95) and the *Michelin Green Guide to Italy* (Michelin, £7.45). If you want to know how Italy works – and what sort of people the Italians really are – William Ward's book *Getting It Right in Italy* (Bloomsbury, £12.99) is a marvellous read.

Of the city guides recommended publications include: the *Everyman Guides to Florence and Venice* (Everyman Library, £16.99 each); *Rome City Guide* (Cadogan Books, £9.99) by Dana Facaros and Michael Pauls; the *Eyewitness Travel Guide to Rome* (Dorling Kindersley, £14.99); and *Florence: The Biography of a City* (Viking, £22.50) by Christopher Hibbert.

If you are looking for hotels, the best of the hotel guides is certainly the *Michelin Red Guide to Italy* which also includes invaluable street plans for the bigger towns and cities.

Specialist travel bookshops in the UK include:

Daunt Books for Travellers
83 Marylebone High Street, London W1 (071-224 2295): Fascinating shop owned and managed by James Daunt where books are arranged geographically.

Stanfords
12-14 Long Acre, London WC2E 9LP (071-836 1321): Stanfords has been serving the needs of the independent traveller since 1851; the management claims that Stanford's 16 staff is ready to offer expert advice on the shop's stock of 20,000 maps and books. Stanford's can also handle inquiries by phone or mail.

Travel Bookshop
13 Blenheim Crescent, London W11 2EE (071-229 5260): New and second-hand books with over 12,000 titles covering guide-books as well as background works on art, history and wildlife – and also fiction. Mail order service: send s.a.e. for special lists. Credit card orders taken on telephone.

Travellers' Bookshop
25 Cecil Court, London WC2N 4EZ (071-836 9132): The shop also has a good selection of new and second-hand travel books.

Waterstones
121-125 Charing Cross Road, London WC2 (071-434 4291): The Charing Cross branch has the best range of travel books, but the other thirteen shops in London and the 87 elsewhere in the UK have a comprehensive range.

PASSPORTS
To enter Italy you do not need the full British passport: the 12 month Visitors' passport available from Post Offices is suffi-cient. However if you take regular holidays abroad, the full 10 year passport available from the Passport Offices listed below is the best value. An application form is available from main post offices. A 32-page passport costs £15; a 48-page passport costs £22.50.

Passport Offices

Liverpool
Passport Office,
5th Floor,
India Buildings,
Water Street,
Liverpool L2 0QZ
051-237 3010

London
Passport Office,
Clive House,
70 Petty France,
London SW1H 9HD
071-279 3434

Newport
Passport Office,
Olympia House,
Upper Dock Street,
Newport,
Gwent NPT 1XA
0633 244500/244292

Peterborough
Passport Office,
Aragon Court,
Northminster Road,
Peterborough PE1 1QG
0733 895 555

Scotland
Passport Office,
3 Northgate,
96 Milton Street,
Cowcaddens,
Glasgow G4 0BT
041-332 0271

Northern Ireland
Passport Office,
Hampton House,
47-53 High Street,
Belfast BT1 2QS
0232 232371

DRIVING LICENCE

You will need to show your UK driving licence before you can hire a car (so will other members of the party if they wish to share the driving). An International Driver's Permit is not necessary.

HEALTH AND INSURANCE

There is no need for any vaccinations or other medical precautions. The only medical precaution necessary is a financial one. You need to have insurance which will not only be sufficient to cover you against medical costs will also offer cover against other routine hazards such as cancellation and theft. If you are driving to Italy consider taking out one the motoring rescue policies such as AA Five Star which will offer assistance if you have an accident or suffer a mechancial breakdown.

TAKING MONEY

For any travel overseas nowadays a credit card is an almost indispensable companion. When we travel as a family, a credit card is our principal means of payment. If you dislike the concept of credit cards (this is understandable!), travellers cheques and Eurocheques will do just as well – but they are a less efficient and more expensive means of paying bills abroad.

We always take a couple of hundred pounds in the local currency as a start as well as a couple of hundred pounds in Sterling as a back-up. Many bills such as hotel bills, car hire charges, petrol etc can be paid directly by credit card. If you need further amounts of local currency these can be obtained from most cash dispensers in Italy by placing your credit card in an automatic cash dispenser. By keying in your PIN number, you can withdraw money. Since these machines occasionally swallow cards for no obvious reason, it may be wise not to travel with one credit card as your sole source of funds.

SAFE TRAVELLING

Ever since the days of the 17th century Grand Tourist, travellers in Italy have been a target for the petty criminal. Happily, most of the crime is non-violent.

Tourists in Rome and other Italian cities are prey to moped-borne handbag snatchers (*scippatori*) who are off with their booty before victims can react. Pickpockets, often gypsy children, operate on buses on the main tourist routes – particularly from Rome station to St Peter's – and in crowded places. Bags can disappear in restaurants and cars can be rifled or stolen, especially if a radio or belongings are left inside.

Italy's black spot is Bari, on the heel of Italy, where handbag-snatching and thieving are so bad that the German authorities have been advising their own tourists to stay away and take ships to Greece from other ports.

It is wise to be careful with valuables like handbags and cameras: keep them across your body in front of you where you can hold them with a protective hand. If you are staying in a hotel, lock your passports, tickets and other non-essential valuables in the hotel safe. Check with the hotel or local tourist office on the areas best avoided day or night.

If you leave items of value in the car, make sure they are locked away in the boot or kept out of sight under a seat.

15

People never leave car radios in their cars in Italy: they nearly all have the sort that you can take out of the car (you frequently see people in cafes and bars with their radio safely on the table in front of them!).

If someone does make a grab for your handbag, do not attempt to fight back. It is better to lose your handbag than your life.

2

GETTING TO ITALY

If you want to get to Italy quickly, then flying is the only choice. If you are put off the idea of air travel because you think you can't afford it, take another look at the prices. Air fares to Italy are not as expensive as you might think (charter fares are a particularly good buy).

Fly/drive packages are less good value. Hiring a car in Italy is probably more expensive than you might have thought (for some reason Italy is one of the most expensive countries in Europe for car hire: see Chapter Three).

If time is less of a consideration, the other options are taking the car, taking the train, taking the car on the train by Motorail or taking a coach.

Flights (Scheduled services)

Year-round flights operate on the following routes:

From	To	Airline
From	*To*	*Airline*
London		
Heathrow	Bologna	Alitalia
Heathrow	Bologna	BA
Gatwick	Florence	Air UK
Gatwick	Florence	Meridiana
Gatwick	Genoa	BA
Heathrow	Milan (Linate)	Alitalia
Heathrow	Milan (Linate)	BA
Gatwick	Naples	BA
Heathrow	Pisa	Alitalia
Heathrow	Pisa	BA
Gatwick	Rome (Fiumcino)	BA
Heathrow	Rome (Fiumcino)	Alitalia
Heathrow	Rome (Fiumcino)	BA

From	To	Airline
Heathrow	Turin	Alitalia
Heathrow	Turin	BA
Heathrow	Venice	Alitalia
Heathrow	Venice	BA
Gatwick	Verona	Meridiana

Birmingham

Birmingham	Milan (Linate)	BA

Manchester

Manchester	Milan (Linate)	BA
Manchester	Rome (Fiumcino)	BA

Connecting flights via Rome

Alitalia can offer onward connecting flights to Catania, Palermo, Lamezia, Reggio Calabria, Bari, Brindisi, Cagliari and Alghero.

Fares

Normal unrestricted air fares are expensive: in the shoulder season, a fully flexible London Heathrow to Milan return which you alter without penalty, for example, costs £416. Buying straight from the airline the cheapest fare, which must be booked and paid for at the same time and requires a Saturday night stay, costs £214.

By buying through what is known in the trade as a 'consolidator', you can make further savings. For example, with Italy Sky Shuttle (081-748 1333) scheduled return fares to Milan are available from £189.

Reservations

Air UK 0345 666777; Alitalia 071-602 7111; British Airways 081-897 4000/0345 222111; Meridiana 071-839 2222.

Italian cheap fare specialists

Campus Travel (071-730 3402); City Jet (071-387 1017); Condor Travel (071-373 0495); Italia nel Mondo (071-834 7651); Italwings (071-287 2117); Italy Sky Shuttle (081-748 1333); Lupus Travel (071-287 1292); STA Travel (071-937 9921); Trailfinders (071-938 3366); Travel 2001 (071-381 5883).

Year-round charter flights

Not many people realise that regular charter flights operate to the main Italian cities year round – at fares much cheaper than the scheduled rates. For example, a return charter fare from Gatwick to Milan is available from Italy Sky Shuttle (081-748 1333) from just £119. Services offered in the Italy Sky Shuttle programme include:

Bologna from Gatwick	**Pisa** Gatwick
Catania Gatwick	**Rome (Ciampino)** Gatwick and Manchester
Milan (Malpensa) Gatwick	**Treviso** Gatwick
Naples Luton	**Venice** Gatwick and Manchester
Palermo Gatwick and Luton	**Verona** Gatwick

DRIVING

With the opening of the Channel Tunnel offering faster crossings (and better value fares), driving to Italy has arguably become a much more attractive proposition. The extensive Continental motorway system means that nearly all the journey can be completed on fast roads (albeit toll roads – but what you lose on the road charges you more than gain on the absence of contra-flows and the other hold ups familiar to travellers on British motorways).

The best place to cross the Channel – whether by ferry or by tunnel – is a short-sea route to Calais (or Boulogne, Dunkerque or Zeebrugge) which offers quick access to the A26 autoroute.

As this is being written before the Channel Tunnel has opened, it is impossible to predict exactly what fares each of the individual operators will be charging in the summer. But given that in January the ferry companies were already facing the prospect of a price war, cross-Channel travellers are certain to benefit from an alluring array of special deals.

How peak July/August 1994 fares and services compare

Route	Operator	Daily sailings	Journey time	Return fare* (4.5m car and 2 adults)
Hull-Rotterdam	North Sea Ferries	1	14 hours	£358
Hull-Zeebrugge	North Sea Ferries	1	14 hours	£358
Felixstowe-Zeebrugge	P&O Ferries	2	5 hours 45 mins 8 hours (night)	£275-£300
Harwich-Hook of Holland	Stena	2	6 hours 30 mins 8 hours 30 mins(night)	£200-£323*
Sheerness-Vlissingen	Olau	2	7 hours 8 hours 30 mins (night)	£198-£236
Ramsgate Dunkerque	Sally	5	2 hours 30 mins	£190-£255
Ramsgate-Oostende	Sally	6	4 hours	£190-£255
Dover-Calais	Hover-speed	8	Seacat 50 mins	£207-£300
		14	Hovercraft 35 mins	£213-£318
Dover-Calais	Stena	25	1 hour 30 mins	£200-£300
Dover-Calais	P&O Ferries	25	1 hour 15 mins	£128-£300
Folkestone-Boulogne	Hover-speed Seacat	5/6	55 mins	£200-£290
Newhaven-Dieppe	Stena	4	4 hours	£216-£296

*Fare for car and up to five passengers. Exact fare depends upon the time of travel: on longer crossings, particularly for night sailings, you may have the additional cost of on board cabin accommodation. Cheaper fares are available for short-break crossings.

The operators
North Sea Ferries 0482 77177
P&O European Ferries 0304 203388
Stena Line 0233 647047
Olau Line 0795 666666
Sally Line 0843-595522
Hoverspeed 0304 240241

Channel Tunnel
Folkestone-Calais   Le Shuttle   £280-£310
Le Shuttle: 0303 271100

Recommended driving routes to Italy
As you can see from the driving times for the recommended routes below, taking your own car to Italy does not take as long as you might have thought since much of the journey is completed on fast roads.

With an early start from Calais it is quite possible to complete the drive to Florence, for example, in one long day's drive. While this may be possible, it is not advisable. The major cause of motorway accidents is tiredness – the boredom induced by long periods of staring ahead at an unchanging highway leads to loss of concentration.

Give yourself two days for the drive and make frequent stops (continental motorways are much better supplied with service areas for petrol and meals – and with general rest areas located in- between the service stations where you can park up to stretch your legs and get a breath of fresh air).

To make the journey easier with children invest in a few good story tapes. *Anne of Green Gables* once took us across France, Martin Jarvis reading *William* stories has preserved our sanity on long drives everywhere (including Australia).

Have food and drink – particularly bottles of mineral water during hot weather. Also you will need local currency for the motorway charges: the pay stations crop with alarming frequency.

To drive on the motorways in Switzerland you require a motorway tax disc which can be bought on the Swiss border for 30 Swiss Francs or from the Swiss tourist office in London (Swiss National Tourist Office, Swiss Centre, New Coventry Street, London W1V 8EE: 071-734 1921; Fax: 071-437 4577) for £14. If you drive on a Swiss motorway without displaying the disc – which lasts for a calendar year – you face an on-the-spot fine of 100 Swiss Francs (£45.50) plus the cost of a disc.

Petrol in Italy is expensive: recent tax increases have made it the most expensive in Europe. You can no longer obtain the petrol coupons which allowed visiting motorists a 15 per cent discount.

Recommended driving routes
Names of places shown in the journey descriptions are the ones you will see on the road signs: remember, for example, that Basle will appear as Bâle (in French) and Basel (in German) – and that in Italian, Florence is Firenze, Milan is Milano and Venice is Venezia.

Michelin recommended route for travelling from Calais to Florence
Total distance 829 miles (1326kms), expected driving time 13 hours 25 minutes (692 miles/1107kms [10hrs 09mins] are on autoroutes: motorway tolls will cost around £10).

Numbers of Michelin maps which cover the route: 989, 988, 51 and 429

	Time	Kms
1	00:00 Calais (2Km)	0000

Take the A16 towards Dunkerque, Béthune
Continue on the A16 for 3Km
Take the A26 towards Reims, Paris, Arras
Continue on the A26 for 264Km

	Time	Kms
2	02:32 (Reims)	0269

At Reims take the A4 towards Metz
Continue on the A4 for 46Km until the Charleville-Mézières exit

	Time	Kms
3	02:57 (Châlons-sur-Marne)	0315

At Châlons take the RD77 for 2.5Km
Next take the RD394 for 39Km
Then the D994 for 8Km

4   03:44 Brabant-le-Roi   0365

Take the D75 for 5Km

5   03:48 Laimont   0370

Take the D994 for 12Km

6   04:00 Bar-le-Duc (1.5Km)   0382

Take the N135 for 13Km

7   04:15 (Ligny-en-Barrois)   0396

Take the N4 for 45Km

8   04:44 (Toul)   0441

Take the A31 (towards Nancy) for 16.5Km

9   04:53 (Nancy)   0458

Take the N4 for 3Km before turning on to
the A33 towards Lunéville, Epinal: proceed
on the A33 for 10Km
Take the A330 towards Epinal and
continue for 6Km

10   05:03 (Flavigny-sur-Moselle)   0477

Take the N57 for 78Km

11   05:51 (Remiremont)   0555

Take the N66 for 78Km

12   06:55 (Mulhouse)   0633

Take the A36 towards Mulhouse for 11.5Km
Then take the A35 towards for 25.5Km
Leave the motorway at the Lörrach and
St-Louis exit

13	07:15 Saint-Louis (3.5Km)	0670
	German Frontier	
14	07:18 (Basel)	0674
	Take the A5 for 4Km	
15	**Swiss Frontier**	
	Continue on the A5 for 1Km Join the N2 for 44.5Km	
16	07:47 (Olten)	0723
	Take the N1 for 10Km Continue on the N2 for 40.5Km	
17	08:16 (Luzern)	0773
	Continue on the N2 for 171Km	
18	09:55 (Lugano)	0944
	Continue on the N2 for 30Km	
19	**Italian frontier**	
	Take the A9 for 32Km towards Milano Join the A8 for 5Km towards Barriera Terrazzano. Take the Tangenziale Oveste for 31Km	
20	10:47 (Milano)	1042
	Take the A1 for 103Km in the direction of Piacenza, Parma	
21	11:41 (Parma)	1145
	Continue on the A1 for 45.5Km	

22   12:04 (Modena)   1191

Continue on the A1 for 33.5Km

23   12:22 (Bologna)   1224

Continue on the A1 for 91.5Km towards Firenze
Take the A11 for 5Km and leave at the Firenze exit

24   13:25 Firenze/Florence (5Km)   1326

**Michelin recommended route for
travelling from Calais to Venice**
Total distance 788 miles (1261kms), expected driving time 13
hours 25 minutes (608 miles/974kms [8hrs 59mins] are on
autoroutes)
   Numbers of Michelin maps which cover the route: 989, 988,
51 and 429

	Time	**Kms**
1	**00:00 Calais (2Km)**	**0000**

Take the A16 towards Dunkerque, Béthune
Continue on the A16 for 3Km
Take the A26 towards Reims, Paris, Arras
Continue on the A26 for 264Km

2   02:32 (Reims)   0269

At Reims take the A4 towards Metz
Continue on the A4 for 46Km until the
Charleville-Mézières exit

3   02:57 (Châlons-sur-Marne)   0315

At Châlons take the RD77 for 2.5Km
Next take the RD394 for 39Km
Then the D994 for 8Km

4   03:44 Brabant-le-Roi   0365

Take the D75 for 5Km

| 5 | **03:48 Laimont** | **0370** |

Take the D994 for 12Km

| 6 | **04:00 Bar-le-Duc (1.5Km)** | **0382** |

Take the N135 for 13Km

| 7 | **04:15 (Ligny-en-Barrois)** | **0396** |

Take the N4 for 45Km

| 8 | **04:44 (Toul)** | **0441** |

Take the A31 (towards Nancy) for 16.5Km

| 9 | **04:53 (Nancy)** | **0458** |

Take the N4 for 3Km before turning on
to the A33 towards Lunéville, Epinal:
proceed on the A33 for 10Km
Take the A330 towards Epinal and
continue for 6Km

| 10 | **05:03 (Flavigny-sur-Moselle)** | **0477** |

Take the N57 for 78Km

| 11 | **05:51 (Remiremont)** | **0555** |

Take the N66 for 78Km

| 12 | **06:55 (Mulhouse)** | **0633** |

Take the A36 towards Mulhouse for 11.5Km
Then take the A35 towards for 25.5Km
Leave the motorway at the Lörrach and
St-Louis exit

| 13 | **07:15 Saint-Louis (3.5Km)** | **0670** |

German Frontier

14	**07:18 (Basel)**	**0674**

Take the A5 for 4Km

15	**Swiss Frontier**	

Continue on the A5 for 1Km
Join the N2 for 44.5Km

16	**07:47 (Olten)**	**0723**

Take the N1 for 10Km
Continue on the N2 for 40.5Km

17	**08:16 (Luzern)**	**0773**

Continue on the N2 for 171Km

18	**09:55 (Lugano)**	**0944**

Continue on the N2 for 28Km

19	**10:11 (Chiasso)**	**0972**

Take Route 2 for 2Km

20	**Italian Frontier**	

Continue on Route 2 for 2Km

21	**10:15 Como (2Km)**	**0976**

Take SS342 for 52Km

22	**11:07 (Bergamo)**	**1030**

Continue for 5Km and join the A4 in the
direction of Briesca, Verona, Vicenza, and
drive for 43Km

23	**11:33 (Brescia)**	**1078**

Continue on the A4 for 60Km

24	**12:04 (Verona)**	**1138**

Continue on the A4 for 80.5Km

25	**12:46 (Padova)**	**1219**

Continue on the A4 for 32.5Km, leaving the motorway at the Mestre, Scorzé exit

26	**13:03 Mestre (3Km)**	**1251**

Take the SS14b for 2Km and the SS11 for 5Km

27	**13:25 Venezia/Venice**	**1261**

MOTORAIL

If you are concerned about the amount of driving involved in taking your car to Italy – or you are worried that your car is not up to the stresses and strains of a long drive – the answer is put the car on the train with Motorail. It certainly isn't a cheap way of travelling (even allowing for the money saved on overnight hotels, motorway tolls and petrol, it is still a formidable expense), but many people are keen on the convenience it offers.

During the summer there are Motorail services from Calais to Bologna, Livorno, Milan and Rome. Fares from Calais to Milan, for example, are £540 return for a car, driver and one passenger: children aged four to 11 are charged £33 return.

For travel to destinations further south in Italy, there are onward rail links from Milan to Naples, Villa San Giovanni and Bari; Bologna to Villa San Giovanni and Bari; and from Florence to Villa San Giovanni. As well as Motorail, French Railways (071-409 3518) at 179 Piccadilly in London can offer information about ferry links from Marseille and Toulon to Sardinia: return fares start at £246 for a car and driver, £94 for additional adults and £57 for children aged four to 11.

TRAIN
With the opening of the Channel Tunnel and the planned introduction of high-speed Eurostar rail services from Waterloo in London to the Gare du Nord in Paris, travelling by rail to Italy should become a more attractive proposition (and hopefully a more economic one). With a three hour train journey from London to Paris – and an eleven hour journey from Paris to Milan – the train ride will still not exactly be rapid. However by travelling overnight it can be made to seem less onerous. However travelling with small children it is probably not the best method of reaching Italy. For further information contact the Victoria International Rail Centre: 071-834 7066.

COACH
Eurolines (071-730 0202) offers regular year-round coach services to Turin, Milan, Bologna, Florence and Rome – and summer only services to Verona, Vicenze, Padua and Venice. A coach departing London at 12.30 in the afternoon arrives in Milan at noon the following day. Fares to Milan cost from £62 for children four to 12; from £99 for passengers under 26; and from £109 for an adult return.

3

GETTING AROUND IN ITALY

TRAINS

Compared with British Rail, the Italian train service is impressively efficient and offers surprisingly good value. The Italian rail service FS *(Ferrovie dello Stato)* features a variety of different trains: from the *locale* services which serve every little station to the high speed ETR 450 high speed trains which operate inter-city trains at a premium rate.

Computer terminals in station concourses offer an at-a-touch guide to services and fares (in English if you wish!). While point-to-point fares are on the whole up to 50 per cent cheaper than equivalent routes in the UK (a one-way adult fare from Milan to Venice, for example, costs around £15), for British holidaymakers the best buy is the 'Travel at Will' rail pass which offers eight days' unlimited travel on the Italian network for £88 (£130 first class) – passes for children under 12 are sold at a 50 per cent discount. For further information contact the Victoria International Rail Centre: 071-834 7066.

AIR

There is a comprehensive network of domestic air services in Italy, however air fares tend to be expensive. Information about services and fares from Alitalia in London 071-602 7111.

FERRIES

The off-shore islands of Italy are largely unknown and unvisited by foreigners. In Chapter 8 we list the main tourist islands, and give brief details for ferry and hydrofoil services. The Italian Tourist Office in London can tell you which companies operate where.

CAR HIRE

Italy is one of Europe's more expensive destinations for hiring a car. Hertz, for example, in its special 'Holiday Saver' programme offers a week's car hire, including unlimited mileage, from £216 for the smallest car – a Fiat Uno.

Car hire companies:
Avis (081-848 8733); Budget (0800 181 181); Europcar (081-950 5050); Hertz (081-679 1799/0345 555 888).

TAXIS

Taxi journeys in Italy tend to be very expensive. Frequently the price shown on the meter bears no relation to the amount you are eventually charged by the driver. Get an idea of what the charge will be before you set off to avoid unpleasant surprises at journey's end.

PUBLIC HOLIDAYS

National public holidays include Epiphany 6 January; Easter Monday; Liberation Day 25 April; Labour Day 1 May; Feast of the Assumption 15 August; All Saints Day 1 November; Christmas Day 25 December; and Boxing Day 26 December.

USING THE TELEPHONE

Public telephones used to be a rare sight in Italy. If you wanted to make a call you used call-boxes in bars which accepted *gettoni* (these old-style pay-phones can be still be seen), or else you made a call from a metered phone in a bar, shop or post office (called in Italian *telefono a scatti;* these also still exist).

But now the streets of Italy are full of pay-phones – particularly the new-style phones which as well as coins accept the Italian SIP (the Italian equivalent of British Telecom) telephone card. Unlike other countries' phone cards – such as the British and French – which are hard plastic cards, the Italian card (*carta telefonica*) is made of thin cardboard and can be bought from vending machines or tobacconists and newspaper stands. They come in L5000 or L10000 units, break off the corner of the card where indicated before putting it arrow-first into the upper slot of the machine (after your call is finished, the card will emerge from the lower slot:, the value of unexpired units is shown in the display window of the phone).

For long-distance or international calls, cards are the most practical method of payment (the biggest value coin that boxes take is L500 and you will need at least L2000 in suitable change for even a modest length call).

When calling back to Britain, first dial 00 (the international access code), followed by 44 (UK code), followed by the local STD area code, but omitting the initial zero. In Italy cheap rate for telephone calls is from 10pm to 8am Monday to Saturday and all day Sunday.

You may find it more convenient to use the UK Direct service. If calling from a pay phone you have to insert a L200 coin (which will be returned to you after the call), dial 172 00 44 – you can then reverse the charges or pay by BT Chargecard if you have one. The number for the local international operator is 15.

ELECTRICITY

Electric current is 220V AC like Britain; unlike Britain plugs are two-pin round-pronged plugs.

4

SELF-CATERING HOLIDAYS

When people think of a self-catering holiday on the Continent, their first thought inevitably has been of France: the land of the gite. France has certainly held sway in this regard for much of the Seventies and all of the Eighties. But now there are signs that France may be facing a self-catering rival. Tuscany is beginning to emerge as a rival to France for the hundreds of thousands of British holidaymakers who are keen to venture further afield.

France's success in self-catering holidays, built on the gite system, began in the 1950s when the French government offered grants to farmers for the restoration of dilapidated buildings. The grants were furnished on condition that the restored properties would be available for holiday lets through the government-controlled gite bureau. Over the next 30 years, more than 30,000 properties came on to the letting market.

This sort of quantity of self-catering properties may sound formidable. But Tuscany can certainly compete on volume. In this one area of Italy, it is estimated that there are around 160,000 farmhouses. The Italian government doesn't need to offer grants or provide other incentives to get these houses restored for holiday lets. In the 1970s, the Germans, the Swiss, the British and others were drawn to Tuscany to snap up dilapidated farmhouses for as little as £5,000.

The property bubble burst at the end of the Seventies when the international community panicked at the widely held belief that Italy was 'going Communist'. When the foreigners stayed away rich Italians filled the breach, buying up Tuscan farmhouses as holiday and weekend homes. The result has been the creation of a huge reservoir of potential self-catering accommodation, most of which has yet to be tapped. At the moment it is estimated that around 5,000 Tuscan houses and apartments are offered for holiday lets.

Significantly, most of the Tuscan properties available for let are of a much higher standard than the French gites. Many of the best Tuscan places have swimming-pools, for example; nearly all are tastefully decorated and elegantly furnished. French gites tend towards the tatty – I've yet to find one that has a decent bed.

The higher standards can be partly explained by the fact that many places are owned by rich style-conscious Italians, Germans or Swiss – or have been restored with an eye to attracting Swiss or German holidaymakers whose standards seem to be rather more exacting than our own. But if the standards are higher, then so are the prices. A French gite holiday is usually an inexpensive one. Tuscan farmhouses do not always come cheap. An average rent starts about £500 a week – some cost up to ten times this amount but experience shows that the British are usually happy to pay extra as long as they feel it is worth it.

Tuscany, like much of the rest of Italy, certainly offers value for money. Eating out is much cheaper than in France, particularly if you are happy to live on pizzas and pasta. The pleasures of the countryside which surrounds Florence and Siena have so far been enjoyed by a rather select British group whose enthusiastic patronage has given the area the nickname of 'Chianti-shire'. These happy few probably hope that the area retains its relative exclusivity. They seem likely to be disappointed. The British self-catering invasion will start at Tuscany. Today Tuscany, tomorrow the rest of Italy.

AGRITURISMO

The Agriturismo is Italy's answer to France's self-catering gites; many places also offer bed and breakfast (like the French chambres d'hotes) and very good value for money. Unfortunately the marketing of Agriturismo in Italy is a little haphazard. The Italian tourist office in London which ought to have information and brochures, is not adequately supplied with either. The two main regions to offer Agriturismo in Italy are Tuscany and Umbria. Tuscany produces the fattest and slickest guide full of colour photographs of the properties on offer. The guide can be bought in bookshops in Italy for L15,000 (£6).

The Tuscan Agriturismo organisations to contact are:

Arezzo:
Agriturist Provinciale, Via G Monaco 80, Cap 52100 Arezzo
(Tel: 0575-300751)

Florence:
Agriturist Provinciale, Piazza S Firenze, 3, Cap 50122, Firenze
(Tel: 055-2396362)

Grosseto:
Agriturist Provinciale, Via D Chiesa, 4 Cap 58100, Grosseto
(Tel: 0564 21010)

Livorno:
Agriturist Provinciale, Via G Marradi 14, Cap 57126, Livorno
(Tel: 0586-812744/7)

Lucca:
Agriturist Provinciale, Viale Barsanti e Matteuci, 55100, Lucca
(0583-332044)

Massa:
Agriturist Provinciale, via M Giuliani 9, Cap 54001, Aulla
(Tel: 0187-421028)

Pisa:
Agriturist Provinciale, Via B Croce, 62, Cap 56100, Pisa
(Tel: 0588-26221)

Pistoia:
Agriturist Provinciale, Via Pacini 45, Cap 51100, Pistoia
(Tel: 0573-21231)

Prato:
Agriturist Provinciale, Via Maria in Castello, 8, Cap 50047
(Tel: 055-20339)

Siena:
Agriturist Provinciale, Via della Sapienza 39, Cap 53100, Siena
(Tel: 0577-46194)

Umbria:
The Umbrian Guide to Agriturismo can be obtained by writing to: Agriturist Umbria, c/o Federubmria Agricoltori, Via Savonarola, 38, 06100, Perugia (Tel: 075-32028/33674; fax 075-32028).

ABRUZZO

Ilios Island Holidays (0403 259788)
Province of Chieti. For example, two weeks in a house sleeping six people and with a private pool costs from £1650 to £3300. Prices are for the property only.

ADRIATIC COAST

Thomson (081-200 8733)
For example, a 14 night holiday at the Elena Apartments located in Cattolica costs from £185 to £355 per person.

APULIA

Long Travel (0694 722193)
Traditional trulli houses in the Itria Valley. Prices range from £160 to £500 per week, per house sleeping up to eight people.

CALABRIA

Long Travel (0694 722193)
Modern villas and apartments near Cirella/Scalea and Tropea from £250 to £500 per week, per house sleeping up to six people.

FLORENCE

1st Roman Breaks (081-660 0082)
One week in a studio apartment for two people in the centre of Florence costs from £380, in the outskirts from £180. Bed linen and towels are provided. The price is for the property only.

International Chapters (071-722 9560)

City centre apartments. For example, a third floor apartment, sleeping four people, in the Palazzo Antellesi which is situated in Piazza Santa Croce, costs £1350 per week.

ISLANDS

Beach Villas (0223 311113)

Elba. An apartment for four people in Seccheto at the western end of Elba's coast costs from £149 to £269 for one week's rental – flights are not included in the price.

Italian Escapades (081-748 2661)

Ischia. Two weeks at the Covo dei Borboni apartments with pool costs from £368 per person, based on four people sharing two bedrooms to £835 per person based on two sharing a studio apartment. Prices include return charter flights.

ITALIAN RIVIERA

Ilios Island Holidays (0403 259788)

Destinations include Bordighiera, close to the French border, one hour's drive from Nice. Country houses and cottages with pools. Two weeks in a house for six people with a private pool costs from £1650 to £3300. A cottage for two people with a shared pool costs from £570 to £810 for two weeks. Prices are for the property only.

LAKES

Auto Plan Holidays (0543 257777)

A 10 day self drive holiday in a two bedroom apartment at Tignale, 3 kms above Lake Garda with access to a private pool costs from £154 to £238 per person. This price includes return ferry and two overnight stops for four people.

Citalia (081-686 5533)

Lake Garda. Prices for 14 nights are £399 to £519 per person. This is based on four sharing and includes return flights to Verona.

37

Eurovillas (0376 561156)
Lake Garda: apartments with pools for two to four people in the lakeside town of Bardolino and on the plateau above the lake range from £380 to £500 per apartment per week. Prices do not include travel.

Magic of Italy (081-748 7575)
Destinations include Lake Garda, Lake Maggiore and Lake Como. The accommodation is apartments, most with pools, some in the grounds of a hotel. Prices range from £407 for four people in a one bedroom apartment on Lake Garda to £864 for two people in a one bedroom apartment on Lake Garda.

Sovereign (0293 599988)
Lake Garda. For example, a seven night stay in an apartment at the Residence Poiano costs from £332 to £421 per person, based on four sharing. Flights from Gatwick are included.

MARCHE

Ilios Island Holidays (0403 259788)
Monte San Martino. Two weeks in a house sleeping six people with a pool costs from £1650 to £3300. Prices are for the property only.

NAPLES AND SURROUNDING REGION

Citalia (081-686 5533)
Sorrento. Prices for 14 nights range from £539 to £869 per person. This price includes breakfast and return air fare to Naples.

Magic of Italy (081-748 7575)
Destinations include Sorrento, Amalfi, Atrani, Ravello and Santa Maria. We offer apartments, mostly with pools, including those in a Residence, in a villa built as a Villa Nobile in 1877 and in a 16th century castle. Prices include return charter flights and return transfers. They range from £296 for four people in a one bedroom apartment in Ravello to £930 for two people in a studio in Sorrento.

Sovereign (0293 599988)
Destinations include Ravello and Maiori. For example, a 14 night stay at the Villa Casale near Ravello costs from £436 to £529 per person, based on four sharing. Flights from Gatwick are included.

PUGLIA

Magic of Italy (081-748 7575)
Apartments in the grounds of a hotel in Cisternino. Prices range from £638 for three people in a one bedroom apartment to £773 for two people in a one bedroom apartment. Prices include return charter flights and unlimited mileage car hire for the duration.

ROME AND SURROUNDING REGION

1st Roman Breaks (081-660 0082)
One week in a studio apartment for two people in the centre of Rome costs from £380, in the outskirts from £180. Bed linen and towels are provided. The price does not include travel.

Ilios Island Holidays (0403 259788)
Situated in Rome, between the Pantheon and the Piazza Navona, this apartment costs £690 per week and sleeps two people.

International Chapters (071-722 9560)
City centre apartments. For example, an apartment sleeping two people located between the Pantheon and Piazza Navona costs £1125 per week.

Vacanze in Italia (07987 426)
Accommodation in Rome itself or short distances away. For example, a first floor flat sleeping two people, halfway between the Vatican City and the ancient Roman historic centre costs £636 per week, all year round.

SARDINIA

Allegro Holidays (0444 248222)
One and two bedroomed apartments with pools along the lido beach of Alghero. Several have services and facilities comparable to a three star hotel. Prices range from £349 to £549 per person for two weeks.

Magic of Italy (081-748 7575)
Destinations include Porto Rafael and Baia Sardinia. Accommodation includes villas and apartments including privately owned villas, villas in the grounds of a hotel and apartments with direct access to the beach. Prices range from £397 for four people in a one bedroom apartment in Baia Sardinia to £1001 for five people in a five bedroom villa in Baia Sardinia. Prices include return charter flights and transfers.

Sardatur Holidays (071-637 0281)
Destinations include Villasimus, Costa Rei, Santa Margherita di Pula and Porto Rotondo. Two weeks in a two bedroom villa including flights and car hire costs from £360 to £595 per person.

Sovereign (0293 599988)
Destinations include Sa Playa, Porto Ottiolu and Santa Teresa di Gallura. For example, a seven night stay at La Marmorata near Santa Teresa di Gallura in a two bedroom apartment for up to five people costs from £383 to £492 per person, flight inclusive.

SICILY

Citalia (081-686 5533)
Taormina. Prices for 14 nights range from £399 to £569 per person, based on four sharing and including return flights to Catania.

Long Travel (0694 722193)
Houses on working farms near Piazza Armeria, Sciacca, Acireale and Riposto from £160 to £500 per week, per house sleeping up to eight people.

Magic of Italy (081-748 7575)

Apartments in Taormina. Prices range from £399 for three people in a one bedroom apartment to £649 for two people in a one bedroom apartment. Prices include charter flights and transfers.

Sunvil Holidays (081-568 4499)

Destinations include Taormina and San Vito lo Capo. Prices for a two bedroom apartment in Taormina range from £412 to £654 per person, including return air fare.

The Sicilian Experience (071-828 9171)

Apartments in Taormina cost from £399 to £599 for two people, flight inclusive for 14 nights.

TUSCANY

Auto Plan Holidays (0543 257777)

Apartments with a pool near Volterra. A two bedroom apartment sleeping four people for 10 days costs from £229 to £269 per person. This price includes ferry, two en route stops and AA five star cover. An extra week's rental is £550.

Beach Villas (0223 311113)

Destinations include Marina di Massa, Massa Cinquale, Lucca, Florence, Pratale and Arezzo. For example, a villa for four people in Marina di Massa, set in a well kept garden with two bikes provided, costs from £299 to £456 per person for 14 nights, flight inclusive.

Blackheath Wine Trails (081-463 0012)

Castello Vicchiomaggio, Greve in Chianti – a wine producing estate in the heart of the Chianti region, offering a range of apartments in the castle. Casa Giotto, a large renovated farmhouse with a private garden. Available throughout the year, all with private facilities and kitchen. Fattoria di Pagliarese, near Castelnuovo Berardenga – in the heart of the rolling Chianti countryside. Excellent family accommodation on a wine producing estate. Large swimming pool. Close to Siena and a comfortable drive to Florence. Prices on request.

Bridgewater's Toscana (061-787 8587)
Inland and coastal properties. For example, a newly-built villa in Marina di Pietrasanta, sleeping seven people costs from £675 to £1150 per week.

CV Travel (071-584 8803)
High quality villas with pools. For example, a pretty farmhouse sleeping six people, 30 minutes by car from Siena, with its own walled garden and swimming pool costs £1355 per week.

Carefree Italy (0689 841900)
Castles, villas and farmhouses. Prices range from £300 to £960 per property, per week.

Citalia (081-686 5533)
Destinations include Florence, Ponte Agli Stolli, Greve, Strove, Lucignano, Castelfiorentino, Policiano, Sarteano and Impruneta. For example, seven nights in Florence costs from £169 to £299 per person, based on four sharing and including air fares. 14 nights in Lucignano ranges from £465 to £575 per person, based on four sharing and including return flights to Pisa or Florence, car hire and a welcome hamper.

Continental Villas (071-497 0444)
Apartments and villas with private pools around Florence, Siena, Lucca and Grosseto. For example, two weeks in a three bedroom apartment costs from £429 to £678 per person, flight inclusive.

Cresta Holidays (061 927 7000)
Destinations featured include San Giuliano (near Pisa), Monteriggioni and Montalcino. The selected villas and apartments are essentially country properties and are therefore situated outside the towns mentioned. All properties have a pool. Prices on request.

Eurovillas (0376 561156)
Destinations featured include Lucca, Bagni di Lucca, Arezzo, Sansepolcro, Pieve S. Stefano and Cortona. Apartments for two to four people inside the walled city of Lucca range from around £275 to £350 per apartment per week. A large ground

floor apartment in a Tuscan manor, sleeping eight people, with a pool costs from £500 to £820 per week.

Hoseasons Holidays Abroad (0502 500555)
Types of accommodation available include apartments, villas, semi and detached houses, mainly centred in the south of Tuscany around the villages of Roccastrada and Sassofortino. A few coastal properties are available. Two weeks in a three bedroomed house near Castiglione costs from £660 to £990 for up to six people. Ferry or air fares are extra.

Ilios Island Holidays (0403 259788)
Destinations include Florence, Siena, Valdichiana, Lake Trasimeno and Monte Argentario. Country homes and cottages with private pools. For example two weeks in a house for six people with a private pool costs from £1650 to £3300. A cottage for two people costs from £570 to £810 for a fortnight. Property prices only.

International Chapters (071-722 9560)
High quality villas with private swimming pools. Prices range from approximately £500 to £5000 per villa, per week.

Invitation to Tuscany (061-775 6637)
Destinations featured include Siena, Casole d'Elsa, San Gimignano and Florence. Invitation to Tuscany offers self-catering accommodation in farmhouses, villas and cottages on a per property, per week price basis, not calculated per person and not including flights though this can be arranged. Property prices range from £240 for a house for five in low season to £3000 for a villa for 10 in high season, with a pool, tennis court, maid and cook service. With car hire and flight the highest cost per person for a fortnight is about £900.

Italian Escapades (081-748 2661)
Destinations include Castellina in Chianti, Castel San Gimignano, Montepulciano, Casole Val d'Elsa and Monteriggioni. Accommodation featured includes a medieval hamlet, 14th century villas, a one bedroom villa surrounding a 10th century watch tower and a renovated medieval castle. Prices for a two week holiday range from £252 per person, based on five people sharing a two bedroom villa to £871 per person,

based on two people sharing a two bedroom villa. Prices include return charter flights.

Italiatour (071-371 1114)
Thirty minutes drive from Florence. Two weeks at the Fattoria La Loggia in an apartment for four people costs from £581 to £927 per person, flight inclusive.

La Bella Toscana (081-422 9218)
Villa and farmhouse accommodation in the little medieval city of San Gimignano which is halfway between Florence and Siena and the surrounding countryside. For example, one week in August in a two bedroomed villa with a swimming pool costs £684. One week in April in a one bedroomed city apartment costs £137. Prices are for property rental only.

Magic of Italy (081-748 7575)
Destinations include Mercatale, Montepulciano, Castra, San Quirico, Monteriggioni, San Gimignano, Certaldo, Impruneta, Radda in Chianti, Piteccio, San Marcello, Porto, Pistoia and San Pancrazio. They offer villas and apartments (mostly with pools) including those in farmhouses, in the grounds of a hotel, in the centre of San Gimignano, in a 16th century house built as a hunting lodge, a 14th century castle, an 18th century castle and in a 13th century manor house on a wine and olive producing estate. Prices include return charter flights and unlimited mileage car hire for the duration. For example, from £359 for four people at I Pini apartments at Impruneta to £1176 for two people in a two bedroom villa at Villa del Monte, near San Gimignano.

Premier Italy (081-390 5554)
A selection of beautifully converted farmhouse properties with swimming pools. For example, two weeks in the Fattoria Canale which is 45 minutes from Pisa costs from £369 to £555 per person, including return air fare and a Group B car for the duration of the holiday. Villa only prices at the above property start from £125 per villa apartment per week.

Rosemary & Frances Villas (071-235 8825)
Villas and apartments. For example, an apartment with a shared swimming pool in a farmhouse in Chianti costs from £725 to £1900. Prices are for the property only.

Sovereign (0293 599988)
Destinations include Casole d'Elsa, Torrita di Siena, San Quirico d'Orcia, San Rocco a Pilli, Pievescola, Colle Val d'Elsa, Pontassieve, San Giorgio, Pelago and Donnini. For example, a fortnight's holiday at the San Lorenzo apartments, situated in a medieval monastery, near Siena, costs from £522 to £779 per person, based on four sharing. Prices include flights and car hire.

Sunvil Holidays (081-568 4499)
Two weeks in a two bedroom apartment in a converted farm building costs from £556 to £644 per person including the return air fare to Florence and a Group C car.

Traditional Tuscany (081-305 1380)
Five estates in the hills east of Florence or further south towards the Umbrian border. For example, a two bedroom cottage near Florence costs from £150 to £180 per person for a fortnight. Travel costs are not included.

Tuscany – from Cottages to Castles (0622 726883)
Siena, Florence, Cortona and Arezzo. Prices are per property, not per person. An apartment for two people in the lowest season can cost £160 per week. A villa for 12 to 16 people in high season can cost £2590 per week.

Tuscany Now (071-272 5469)
Villas, farmhouses and apartments with swimming pools. Prices range from £231 for a one bedroom apartment to £4000 for a six bedroom villa for one week. Prices are for accommodation only.

Vacanze in Italia (07987 426)
Properties inland and on the Tuscan coast. For example, Il Casello Vico D'Arbia near Siena is a recently converted property set on a farm, with a swimming pool, sleeping eight people, which costs from £1780 per week in mid season to £2298 for a fortnight in high season.

Veronica Tomasso Cotgrove (071-267 2423)
Apartments, and farmhouses all with swimming pools. A house sleeping eight to ten people with a private pool

costs from £700 to £2400 per week, per property and excluding air fares.

Villa Fillinelle (0604 720242)
Villas, apartments and houses situated in many areas of Tuscany including San Gimignano, Greve, Marina di Massa, and Lamporecchio. Two weeks at an apartment in Villa del Monte sleeping four people costs from £470 upwards, depending on the size of apartment needed. Travel arrangements can also be made, if required.

Villas Argentario (081-994 2956)
Destinations include Monte Argentario on the Tuscany coast and Florence. Prices range from £400, for a fortnight in an apartment sleeping two to four people to £3000 for an apartment sleeping 14 people. Also offered are apartments in the castle and estate of Castello di Montefugno, near Florence, which is partly 15th century and earlier. Until recently it was the Sitwell home in Italy. It has now been bought by Italians and sensitively converted into 20 apartments with all the original features, including frescoes, fireplaces, elaborate ceilings, with mostly period furniture but also with central heating. Prices range from £450 for an apartment sleeping two to £2200 for an apartment sleeping eight. All prices are per property.

UMBRIA

CV Travel (071-584 8803)
Villas ranging in size from those suitable for two people to more spacious properties suitable for up to 16 people. All villas have swimming pools and many have tennis courts. Prices range from £430 per week for a small villa for two to £1975 per week for a villa sleeping up to 14 people.

Carefree Italy (0689 841900)
Castles, villas and farmhouses. Prices range from £300 to £960 per property, per week.

Citalia (081-686 5533)
Gubbio. Prices range from £355 to £515 per person, based on

four sharing, and including return flights to Pisa or Florence, car hire and a welcome hamper.

Ilios Island Holidays (0403 259788)
Destinations include Citta della Pieve, Orvieto, Todi, Amelia and the Perugia area. Country houses and cottages with private pools. Two weeks in a house for six with a private pool costs from £1650 to £3300. A cottage for two people costs from £570 to £810 for a fortnight. Prices are for the property only.

International Chapters (071-722 9560)
High quality villas with private swimming pools. Prices range from £500 to £5000 per villa, per week.

Italiatour (071-371 1114)
Destinations include Gubbio, Mantignana and Umbertide. For example, two weeks in an apartment for four people at the Palazzo Contessa in Gubbio costs from £370 to £499 per person, flight inclusive.

Magic of Italy (081-748 7575)
Destinations include Piegaro and Assisi. Our accommodation is mostly apartments with pools, including those in converted farmhouses or in the grounds of an hotel or in a hunting lodge. Prices include return charter flights and unlimited mileage car hire for the duration. They range from £386 for five people in a two bedroom apartment in Piegaro to £896 for two people in a two bedroom apartment near Assisi.

Rosemary & Frances Villas (071-235 8825)
Villas with private swimming pools near Citta di Castello cost from £1450 to £3300 for a fortnight. Prices are for property only.

Sovereign (0293 599988)
Apartments situated near Lake Trasimeno. For example, a fortnight's holiday at the Residence Castiglione costs from £489 to £693 per person, based on four sharing. Flights from Gatwick and car hire are included in the price.

Tuscany – from Cottages to Castles (0622 726883)
Perugia. Prices are per property and not per person. An apartment for two people in the lowest season can cost £160 per

week. A villa for 12 to 16 people in the highest season can cost up to £2590 per week.

Tuscany Now (071-272 5469)
Villas, farmhouses and apartments in farmhouses with swimming pools. Prices range from £231 to £4000 for one week. Prices are for accommodation only.

Vacanze in Italia (07987 426)
Traditional farmhouses and villas. For example, a penthouse in the Palazzo Sbaraglini Assisi, converted from a loggia and sleeping four to five people ranges in price from £408 to £468 for one week.

Veronica Tomasso Cotgrove (071-267 2423)
Farmhouses, historic houses and even a castle. For example, a restored farmhouse dating back to the 14th Century, situated 8 kms from Todi, sleeping eight people with a swimming pool, telephone, central heating, washing machine and a dishwasher costs from £800 to £1350 per week. This price is per property.

VENICE AND THE VENETO

Citalia (081-686 5533)
Gigi apartments. Prices for seven nights start from £169 in low season to £299 in high season. The price is per person and is based on four people sharing, and includes return flights.

Cosmosair (061 480 5799)
Torino Apartments in Lido di Jesolo, 100 metres from the beach. Two weeks for four adults in a one bedroomed apartment costs from £219 to £389 per person, flight inclusive.

Ilios Island Holidays (0403 259788)
Two apartments in Venice situated between the Rialto and the Piazza San Marco cost £1350 per week and sleep three to four people.

International Chapters (071-722 9560)
City centre apartments. For example, a first floor apartment

around the corner from La Fenice Theatre sleeping two to four people costs £680 per week.

Magic of Italy (081-748 7575)
Apartments in a central position in Verona. Prices include return charter flights and transfers and range from £502 for four people in a one bedroom apartment to £1227 for two people in a two bedroom apartment.

Rosemary & Frances Villas (071-235 8825)
A town house in Venice near San Angelo costs from £1300 to £1700 for two weeks. The price is for the property only.

Venetian Apartments (081-878 1130)
City centre apartments. For example, two weeks in a two bedroom apartment on the Giudecca costs from £380 to £465 per person, flight inclusive.

ALL OVER ITALY

Gordon Overland (0228 26795)
Properties throughout Italy from many sources. Main areas are Tuscany, Umbria, Rome and Lombardy. For example, a villa in Tuscany for a family of four costs around £297 per person, including flights.

Interhome (081-891 1294)
3000 properties for rent throughout Italy. The majority are situated in Tuscany and Liguria. For example, a renovated farmhouse in Fosdinovo, west of La Spezia and nine kms from Sarzana, with a private swimming pool and sleeping up to eight people costs from £583 per week. This price is for the property rental only.

International Services USA Inc (06/3600-0018/0019)
Villas, farmhouses and apartments in each province. Properties are also in or near all key cities and towns. Weekly prices range from approximately £500 to £2000 per property, depending on the season, type of accommodation and number of persons in the group.

HOUSE SWAPPING

One of the most difficult problems about holidays is finding the right accommodation, particularly if you have children. Not only are hotels or self-catering apartments rarely suitable or particularly comfortable for families, they hardly ever offer a genuine view of life in the place where you are staying. Wouldn't it be much better to stay in a real home on holiday, to have the normal comforts and luxuries of domestic life: a washing machine, proper sized rooms and a fully equipped kitchen. And to stay amongst real people, not other holiday-makers from your own country.

One answer is house-swapping; exchanging your home for a couple of weeks or more with another family. With an exchange, not only will you get the use of the other family's house, and perhaps also their car, you will also gain admission to the local community. It seems a good idea, but what of the pitfalls? How do you find people to swap with, how do you arrange the swap, how can you be sure your house will be looked after properly, does your home insurance cover such exchanges?

How to swap

The most straightforward way to arrange an overseas or UK swap is to advertise, for a fee, in a house-swapping directory: the biggest is produced by Intervac. Several directories are published in Britain:

Home Base Holidays

7 Park Avenue, London N13 5PG (081-886 8752): Specialises in home swaps with families in the US and Canada. It produces three brochures a year; membership costs £32.

Homelink International

Linfield House, Gorse Hill Road, Virginia Water, Surrey GU25 4AS (0344 842642): One of the biggest home swapping agencies with more than 16,000 registered members in over 50 countries, it publishes six catalogues during the year. Annual membership is £47.

Intervac International Home Exchange

3 Orchard Court, North Wraxall, Chippenham, Wiltshire SN14 7AD (0225 892208): Over 9000 members and three directories a year (with a late-exchange service). Annual membership is £65.

You could also consider trying to arrange a swap through personal contacts: friends or friends of friends who live overseas. If the company you work for, for example, has overseas offices and representatives, perhaps you might be able to organise a swap through them.

The possible dangers
According to the home swapping agencies, home swapping disasters hardly ever happen: the only problem is likely to be that the person you're planning to swap with has to back out because of family illness or the death of a relative.

The agencies report that families are very good about paying for any breakages or any damage they cause. Intervac says the fact that there is no rental fee involved seems to make people especially careful about how they treat the house where they are unminded guests. But if you are especially houseproud however then house swapping may not suit you. If you wish to swap your house, it helps if it is in a place well known as a tourist area: in London, for example, or Oxford – but location isn't always important.

Insurance:
You must tell your house and car insurance company about the exchange: if you don't, it may affect your cover.

Further information:
The Consumers Association magazine *Which?* (November 1986) has a very useful guide to house swapping, and advice on making the necessary arrangements. Back numbers of *Which?* are available from reference libraries.

5

HOTEL HOLIDAYS

Curiously, the Italian hotel industry has evolved in quite a different way from neighbouring France. Twenty years ago France was practically a hotel chain-free country: here the small hotelier reigned. Variations on the classic restaurant-avec-chambres theme, where granny manned the desk, mum and dad ran the kitchen and where the rest of the family weighed in as waiters, waitresses and chambermaids.

Then it would have been impossible to foresee the change that was to come. Visit even the smallest French town today and you will see that France has gone chain hotel mad. Budget motels, low-cost hotels, you name it the French have it. The small hotelier is rapidly becoming an endangered species.

So far, Italy has resisted the rise of the motel chain. Here the *pensione*, the small independent hotel still holds sway. Unhappily the absence of competition has done little for value for money. In the main tourist destinations like Venice and Florence, for example, you are unlikely to find even a modest room for less than £30 a night – a reasonable room with en suite facilities will start at around £50 a night (compare this with the French motel chains that offer rooms from less than £20 a night).

A number of agencies in the UK claim to be able to offer Italian hotel accommodation at a discount. These include:

Accommodation Line Ltd
PO Box 1877, London W10 4ZE (081-964 2509; fax 081-964 2088): 'We specialise in the booking of good value for money hotels, bed and breakfast places and Italian Pensioni. We have personally visited all the hotels we feature.' Double rooms in Venice start at £19; Florence from £19; and Venice from £18.

Hotel Promotions Services Ltd
(081-446 0126): Booking service to more than 500 hotels in Italy.

'Free style travel for the independently minded. The leading UK reservations agency for hotels in over 200 Italian locations – cities, seaside, lakes and mountains.' Double rooms from £29 per night.

Italberghi
35 Bimport, Shaftesbury, Dorset (0747 55855; fax 0747 51207): Hotels in Italian cities, the Lakes and the seaside. Double rooms from £19 per night.

Room Service
42 Riding House Street, London W1P 7PL (071-636 6888; fax 071-636 6002). 'The majority of hotels we deal with are family-run properties, personally directed by the owners. We specialise in the one to three star categories, also known as pensiones, which we believe offer the best combination of location, value for money and charm.' The company says it is able to confirm bookings within 24 hours. In Milan, for example, it offers double rooms from £28 per night; Verona from £30 per night; Siena from £29 per night; Pisa from £16 per night; Bologna from £28 per night; Florence from £18 per night; Rome from £20 per night; and Venice from £18 per night.

OPERATORS OFFERING HOTEL-INCLUSIVE PACKAGES

ADRIATIC COAST

Airtours (0706 260000)
Cattolica and Rimini. For example, a 14 night stay on half-board at the Hotel King in Cattolica costs from £279 to £519 per person, flight inclusive.

DOLOMITES

Inntravel (0439 71111)
Destinations include Kastelruth, San Michele, Appiano and Girlan. For example, a three night stay at the three star castle hotel in San Michele which has an outdoor swimming pool costs from £178 to £206 per person, staying on a bed and breakfast basis. This is a self-drive holiday.

ISLANDS

Italian Escapades (081-748 2661)
Capri, Ischia and Elba. Hotels range from four star to five star. For example, a two week holiday at the Hotel Park Michelangelo on Ischia staying on a bed and breakfast basis costs from £523 per person, based on two sharing. A two week holiday in high season staying at the Hotel Europa Palace on Capri on half-board costs up to £5805 per person. Prices include return charter flights.

LAKES

Airtours (0706 260000)
Destinations include Limone, Riva/Torbole, Malcesine, Bardolino and Garda – all on Lake Garda. For example, a 14 night stay at the Hotel Capri in Bardolino costs from £349 to £499 per person, on a bed and breakfast basis. The hotel offers a free bike per room for house guests and others are available for hire.

Auto Plan Holidays (0543 257777)
Lake Garda and Lake Como. For example, a 10 day self drive holiday to Lake Como in August, staying at a two star hotel with a pool costs £389 per person, based on two sharing. The price includes half-board, ferry fares and an overnight stop.

Citalia (081-686 5533)
Two to four star hotels in the following areas: Lake Maggiore, Lake Como and Lake Garda. For example, 14 nights at the three star Bellevue San Lorenzo in Malcesine on Lake Garda costs from £649 to £855 per person, including half-board and return flights to Verona.

Cosmosair (061 480 5799)
14 nights at the Hotel Garda on Lake Garda costs from £419 to £539 per person on half-board, flight inclusive.

Italian Escapades (081-748 2661)
Hotels range from two star to five star de luxe. For example, two weeks in low season at the Hotel Villa Smeralda on Lake

Garda on half-board costs £480 per person, based on two sharing. Two weeks in high season at the Grand Hotel Villa Serbelloni in Bellagio on half-board costs £1549 per person, based on two sharing. Prices include return charter flights.

Owners Abroad Travel (0293 554455)
Destinations include Lake Garda and Lake Maggiore. For example, a seven night half-board package at the Hotel Villaminta in Stresa, on Lake Maggiore costs from £342 to £381 per person, including return air travel from London and Manchester. A 14 night twin centre holiday which combines Lake Garda with the Venetian Riviera is also offered. Prices range from £373 to £474 per person staying on a half-board basis, flight inclusive.

Page & Moy (0533 524433)
10 nights by air from Heathrow to Lake Garda and the Dolomites. Accommodation is in two and three star hotels and is on a half-board basis. The cost of the holiday is £499 per person. Optional excursions are offered to Venice and Verona.

Portland Holidays (071-388 5111)
Lake Garda. For example, two weeks at the three star Hotel Venezia which is close to the lake shore costs from £423 to £495 per person, on half-board, flight inclusive.

Sunvil Holidays (081-568 4499)
A two week bed and breakfast stay costs £620 per person at the Hotel Primavera in Stresa. A two week holiday on half-board at the Hotel Cannero on Lake Maggiore costs £1095 per person. Both prices are flight inclusive.

The Travel Club of Upminster (0708 225000)
Lake Garda, Lake Como and Lake Orta. One week at the Hotel San Rocco which was originally a convent, situated on Lake Orta costs from £784 to £798 per person on a half-board basis. One week at the Hotel Don Pedro on the eastern shore of Lake Garda costs from £348 to £438 per person, on half-board.

Thomson (081-200 8733)
For example, a 14 night half-board holiday to Lake Garda staying at the Hotel Idania, Bardolino costs from £1123 to £1524

for a family of three. Activities available in the resort include windsurfing, horseriding, water skiing, tennis and pedalos.

NAPLES AND SURROUNDING REGION

Airtours (0706 260000)
Sorrento. For example, a 14 night stay on half-board at the Hotel Eden costs from £379 to £539 per person, flight inclusive.

At Home in Italy (081-852 0069)
Sorrentine Peninsula. Three to five star hotels. For example, two weeks in Amalfi costs from £210 to £1260 per person on half-board, including air fare.

Citalia (081-686 5533)
Two to five star hotels in the following destinations: Sorrento, Positano, Ravello, Maiori, Amalfi and Paestum. For example, 14 nights at the Imperial Hotel Tramontano, a four star hotel in Sorrento costs from £529 to £729 per person on a half-board basis, flight inclusive.

Cosmosair (061 480 5799)
14 nights on half-board at the three star Hotel Milton in Sorrento costs from £398 to £519 per person, flight inclusive.

Enterprise (061-745 7000)
The Neapolitan Riviera – Sorrento, Massalubrense and Amalfi. For example, a two week stay at the three star Hotel Maria in Massalubrense costs from £369 to £535 per person, on half-board, flight inclusive.

Italian Escapades (081-748 2661)
Resorts featured include Sorrento, Positano, Amalfi, Ravello and Maiori. Hotels range from three star to five star. A two week holiday ranges in price from £327 per person staying at the Hotel Parsifal in Ravello on a bed and breakfast basis to £2025 per person staying at the Hotel Excelsior Vittoria in Sorrento on half-board. Prices include return charter flights.

Owners Abroad Travel (0293 554455)
Sorrento. A seven night half-board package at the Hotel

Settimo in Sorrento costs from £276 to £343 per person, including return air travel from London and Manchester.

Page & Moy (0533 524433)
14 nights by air from Gatwick to the Sorrento Peninsula. Accommodation is at three star family run hotels in Massalubrense and Marina di Camerota and is on a half-board basis. Prices range from £499 to £569 per person. Optional excursions to Pompeii, Capri and the Amalfi Coast are available.

Skybus Holidays (071-373 6055)
Sorrento. For example, a stay at the three star Hotel Gardenia costs from £26 to £34 per person, per night, based on two people sharing and including half-board. Flights cost from £169 to £199 per person for a charter flight and from £209 to £275 per person for a scheduled flight.

Sovereign (0293 599988)
Destinations include Sorrento, Amalfi and Maiori. For example, a fortnight's holiday at the five star Hotel Santa Caterina in Amalfi costs from £861 to £1211 per person staying on a bed and breakfast basis, with two sharing. Flights from Gatwick and Manchester are included in the price.

Thomson (081-200 8733)
In Sorrento, for example, 14 nights at the Hotel Conca costs from £417 to £534 per person on a half-board basis, flight inclusive.

ROME AND SURROUNDING REGION

At Home in Italy (081-852 0069)
Gulf of Gaeta. Formia, Sperlonga and Gaeta are all on the sea but offer medieval architecture, good shopping, markets, wonderful scenery and excursions. Not known to the English. Prices range from £246 to £526 per person on half-board, including air fare to Rome.

Sunvil Holidays (081-568 4499)
A seven night bed and breakfast stay at the Hotel Erdarelli

costs from £429 per person, including air travel and based on two people sharing.

SARDINIA

Allegro Holidays (0444 248222)
Mostly three and four star seaside hotels with pools in or near Alghero. Prices range from £199 per person for seven nights with bed and breakfast accommodation to £849 per person for 14 nights with half-board.

At Home in Italy (081-852 0069)
Prices range from £294 to £441 per person for two weeks on half-board and including air fare to Olbia.

Citalia (081-686 5533)
A selection of accommodation at The Forte Village. For example, 14 nights ranges from £1199 to £1955 per person. The price includes half-board, free beach facilities, tennis, aerobics, evening entertainment and return flights to Cagliari.

Italian Escapades (081-748 2661)
Destinations include the Forte Village, Santa Margherita di Pula, Castiadas, Chia and Puntaldia. A two week holiday ranges in price from £567 per person staying at the Hotel Mare Pineta in Santa Margherita di Pula on half-board to £2733 per person staying at the Forte Village on half-board. Prices include return charter flights.

Sardatur Holidays (071-637 0281)
Destinations include Santa Margherita di Pula, Cagliari, Alghero and Porto Rotondo. Two weeks in a three star hotel on half-board costs from £640 to £1225 per person, including flights.

SICILY

Citalia (081-686 5533)
A selection of two to five star hotels in Taormina and Taormina beach. For example, 14 nights at the four star Villa Paradiso

costs from £734 to £844 per person. This includes half-board, complimentary use of the tennis courts for 45 minutes a day, fruit and wine in room on arrival and return flights to Catania.

Italian Escapades (081-748 2661)
Destinations include Taormina, Cefalu, Giardini Naxos and Palermo. Hotels range from two star to five star. For example, two weeks in low season at the Hotel Villa Carlotta in Taormina staying on a bed and breakfast basis costs £455 per person based on two sharing. Two weeks in high season at the Hotel Villa Igeia in Palermo on bed and breakfast costs £1599 per person, based on two sharing. Prices include return charter flights.

Long Travel (0694 722193)
Mostly three star hotels in Palermo, Taormina, Agrigento and Siracusa from £30 to £52 per person per night.

Sunvil Holidays (081-568 4499)
A 14 night bed and breakfast stay in Taormina ranges from £512 per person at the Villa Schuler to £1799 per person at the San Domenico Palace. Prices include return air fares and transfers and are based on two people sharing.

The Sicilian Experience (071-828 9171)
All categories of hotel offered from two star to five star all over Sicily. Prices range from £450 to £1600 per person for 14 nights including flights.

TUSCANY

At Home in Italy (081-852 0069)
Three and four star hotels chosen for their central position or scenery. Destinations include Montepulciano, Siena and Cortona. Two weeks on half-board ranges from around £250 to £600 per person, flight inclusive.

Auto Plan Holidays (0543 257777)
San Gimignano: a ten day self drive holiday at the three star Hotel Renaie costs from £383 to £411 per person on a bed and breakfast basis. The hotel has a good size swimming pool in

the garden and is set on a hill surrounded by vineyards and olive trees.

CV Travel (071-584 8803)
Four star hotels near Siena, Florence and the small town of Colle di Val D'Elsa. For example, four nights at the Hotel Villa Arceno, near Siena, which lies within a private estate of 1000 hectares costs from £497 to £555 per person, on a bed and breakfast basis, flight inclusive.

Citalia (081-686 5533)
Destinations include San Gimignano, Radda, Lucignano and Siena. For example 14 nights at the three star Villa Miranda in Radda costs from £819 to £899 per person on a half-board basis, flight inclusive.

Italian Escapades (081-748 2661)
Destinations include Viareggio, Forte dei Marmi and Lido di Camaiore on the Tuscan coast. For example, a two week holiday ranges in price from £431 per person, staying at the Hotel Residence Regina in Viareggio on a bed and breakfast basis to £1859 per person, staying at the Hotel Augustus Lido in Forte dei Marmi on half-board. Prices include return charter flights.

Page & Moy (0533 524433)
Accommodation is typically in family run three to four star hotels and usually on a half-board basis. Typical duration is ten nights including seven in a rural area, for example, a hill top town, and three in a major city, for example, Rome, Florence or Venice. Prices range from £479 to £599 per person, flight inclusive.

Skybus Holidays (071-373 6055)
Destinations on the Tuscan coast including Lido di Camaiore, Marina di Pietra Santa and Viareggio are offered. Hotel costs and flights are priced separately so the length of stay is up to the customer. For example, one night at the Hotel Rialto Suisse in Lido di Camaiore costs from £38 to £48 per person, based on two people sharing and including half-board. Flights cost from £169 to £189 per person for a charter flight and from £279 to £329 per person for a scheduled flight.

Sovereign (0293 599988)
Destinations include Donnini, Casole d'Elsa, San Gimignano and Castellina in Chianti. For example, a seven night stay at the Hotel Gemini in Casole d'Elsa costs from £512 to £570 per person, based on two sharing.

Sunvil Holidays (081-568 4499)
Destinations include Volterra, Florence, San Gimignano, Pistoia and Lucca. For example, a seven night bed and breakfast stay at the three star Hotel La Luna in Lucca costs from around £539 to £614 per person, including return air fare and car hire.

UMBRIA

At Home in Italy (081-852 0069)
Destinations include Perugia, Gubbio and Assisi. Three and four star hotels are used and are either in a central position or chosen for their views. Prices on application.

Italian Escapades (081-748 2661)
Destinations include Perugia, Bosco, Cenerente, Spoleto, Assisi and Gubbio. For example, two weeks in low season at the Country House Hotel in Assisi on a bed and breakfast basis costs £528 per person, based on two sharing. Two weeks in high season at the Hotel Brufani in Perugia on a bed and breakfast basis costs £1011 per person, based on two sharing. Prices include return charter flights.

Page & Moy (0533 524433)
Seven nights by air from Heathrow. One night in Rome and six nights in Umbria. Accommodation is in three and four star hotels and is on a half-board basis. Prices range from £479 to £499 per person. This includes excursions to Urbino, Perugia and Assisi, and a sightseeing tour of Rome.

Sunvil Holidays (081-568 4499)
Destinations include Perugia, Gubbio and Orvieto. For example, a two week bed and breakfast stay at the Hotel Signa in Perugia costs from £730 per person, including return air fare and car hire.

VENICE AND THE VENETO

Cosmosair (061 480 5799)
14 nights on half-board at the three star Hotel Harris in Lido di Jesolo costs from £298 to £449 per person, flight inclusive.

Sunvil Holidays (081-568 4499)
A seven night stay at the La Fenice Hotel on a bed and breakfast basis costs around £676 per person, flight inclusive. This price is based on two people sharing.

Thomson (081-200 8733)
For example, in Lido di Jesolo, 14 nights at the Hotel Acapulco costs from £281 to £437 per person on a half-board basis, flight inclusive.

ALL OVER ITALY

AA Driveaway (0256 493878)
Hotel touring holidays. Hotels and ferry crossings may be booked in advance or there is the option to book only the ferry and take nightly vouchers for your hotel accommodation. For example, one night at the Novotel in Bologna on a bed and breakfast basis costs from £92 to £136 per person, based on two people sharing and including ferry crossings. Extra nights cost £43 per person.

Abercrombie & Kent (071-730 9600)
Destinations include the Italian Lakes, the Dolomite mountain ranges, Venice and the Veneto, Tuscany, Umbria, Rome, Florence, Naples and Campania, and Sicily. For example, a seven night stay at the Hotel Flora in Venice costs from £638 to £733 per person on a bed and breakfast basis, flight inclusive.

Cosmosair (061 480 5799)
Two centre holidays by air. For example, three nights in Rome combined with 11 nights in Sorrento costs from £349 to £509 per person. Seven nights in either Lake Garda or Lido di Jesolo combined with a seven night Mediterranean cruise costs from £729 to £809 per person.

Gordon Overland (0228 26795)

A full range of hotels throughout Italy. For example, seven nights on half-board in Sicily costs from £410 per person, including flights. A week near Portofino on the Italian Riviera at a three star hotel costs around £439 per person on half-board, flight inclusive.

HPS Hotels Direct (081-446 0126)

Two to five star hotels in every region. For example, one night at the two star Hotel Centro in Florence costs from £20 per person staying on a bed and breakfast basis. A one night stay at the three star Hotel Ala in Venice costs from £39 per person on a bed and breakfast basis. Air inclusive packages are not offered.

Italberghi (0747 55855)

Owner-managed hotels in major cities, Tuscany and on the Lakes. For example, a stay in the Albergo Villa Schuler in Taormina, Sicily which is surrounded by terraced gardens and has views of Mount Etna and the Bay of Naxos costs from £16 to £24 per person, per night, based on two sharing and including breakfast. There is a minimum stay of three nights.

Italiatour (071-371 1114)

Lake resorts, beach resorts and multi-centre holidays. For example, a two centre holiday which combines Sorrento and Capri costs from £746 to £1141 per person on half-board, flight inclusive, for two weeks.

Liaisons Abroad (071-384 1122)

Hotels range from one to five star and are sold on a per night basis. For example, in Venice prices range from £54 to £180 per room, per night, inclusive of continental breakfast.

Magic of Italy (081-748 7575)

Destinations include Naples and the Amalfi coast, Sicily, Puglia, Sardinia, Liguria and Tuscany. Prices range from £399 for two people in a twin room on a bed and breakfast basis at the Hotel Parsifal in Ravello to £3661 for two people in a twin room on half-board at Romazzino, Costa Smeralda in Sardinia. Prices include return charter flights and transfers.

Premier Italy (081-390 5554)
All types of hotels including small, family-run hotels, Agriturismo and country house hotels. A seven night stay on a bed and breakfast basis in the Parsifal Hotel in Ravello on the Amalfi coast, costs from £279 to £383 per person, including return flights to Naples and transfers on arrival and departure.

Room Service (071-636 6888)
Hotels from one to three star. For example, a fortnight's accommodation in Venice ranges from £210 to £686 per person. Air fares are not included. Rooms in private houses are also offered. For example, a room with its own bathroom in a private villa in Tuscany costs from £23 to £30 per person, per night. Breakfast is included.

6

SPECIAL INTEREST HOLIDAYS

A selection of operators who offer activity and special interest holidays: everything from a nine day volcano hike in Sicily to a tour of wine cellars in Chianti.

ADVENTURE HOLIDAYS

Exodus (081-675 5550)
An accompanied two week itinerary based on bed and breakfast accommodation staying in Siena, Florence, the Apennine Mountains, Cinque Terre and Lucca. The holiday costs from £760 to £820 per person, flight inclusive.

Explore Worldwide (0252 319448)
A nine day volcano hike in Sicily and the Aeolian Islands. 'We plan to climb three living volcanoes – Vulcano, Stromboli and Mount Etna.' The ascents are graded as moderate to strenuous. The group size is 12 to 14. Accommodation comprises hotels for three nights, a bivouac for one night and dorm-style in a mountain refuge for three nights. The price is £595 per person, flight inclusive.

ARCHAEOLOGY

Andante Travels (0980 610555)
Destinations include Pompeii, Sicily and Rome. For example, the Sicilia Antiqua tour which visits the great sites of classical Sicily with a lecturer and tour manager costs from £1182 per person for 11 days. The price includes half-board accommodation, picnics/lunches, coach travel and return air travel.

Page & Moy (0533 524433)
Seven nights by air from Gatwick to Pompeii, Paestum and
Herculaneum. The tour also includes trips to Cumae and
Pozzuoli. The base for the tour is Sorrento and accommodation
is on a half-board basis at the four star Hotel de la Ville. Prices
range from £775 to £825 per person.

Art & Architecture Tours

Martin Randall Travel (081-742 3355)
Destinations include Venice, Rome, Florence and Siena. For
example, a six day trip to Venice accompanied by a lecturer
costs £640 per person, flight inclusive. Accommodation is at
the four star Albergo Cavaletto e Doge Orseolo, close to Piazza
San Marco. The tour includes visits to the 11th century basilica
of San Marco, the Doge's Palace, the church of San Zaccaria,
the Renaissance churches of S. Giovanni Crisostomo and S.
Maria dei Miracoli and the Galleria dell'Accademia. Groups
are of between 10 and 22 participants.

Page & Moy (0533 524433)
Eight nights by air from Heathrow to Sicily. Accommodation is
at the Hotel Carlton Riviera in Cefalu and is on a half-board
basis. The trip includes excursions to see Doric temples,
Roman mosaics and Norman, Renaissance and Baroque architecture. Prices range from £795 to £850 per person.

Art History Tours

Andante Travels (0980 610555)
For example, an eight day tour to Venice with an art historian
who lives and works there, costs from £977 per person. This
includes half-board accommodation, vaporetti rides and return
air travel.

Anglo-Italian Study Tours (071-482 3767)
Six day house-party study holidays based near Lucca in
Tuscany. Sites of major interest are visited and lectures are
given by Dr Edward Chaney, a well known art historian and
writer. Prices, including all entrance fees to galleries and

museums and the six days' accommodation and half-board, range from £675 to £765 per person. Air travel is not included.

Fine Art Travel (071-437 8553)
Destinations include Rome, Ravenna, Urbino and Venice. For example, a seven night holiday to Rome which includes a private visit to the Sistine Chapel costs £1850 per person, including half-board accommodation and air travel.

Prospect Music and Art Tours (081-995 2151)
Cultural weekends and short breaks to Venice, Florence and Rome. For example, the Dawn of the Renaissance tour to Florence accompanied by a guide who will take an introductory walk to some of the main monuments, costs from £495 to £525 per person, on a bed and breakfast basis. Accommodation is at the five star Hotel Villa Medici which was once an 18th century palace. Prospect will provide detailed . t historical notes, but only part of the weekend is structured.

BATTLEFIELD TOURS

Holts' Battlefield Tours (0304 612248)
The three tours in 1994 will be flown on scheduled airlines. The prices include everything except lunch. The Ancient History in Southern Italy tour is based in the Alpha Hotel, Sant Agnello, New Sorrento and costs £669 per person, based on two sharing. The Cassino 50th Anniversary tour is also based at the Alpha Hotel and costs £659 per person, based on two sharing. The Break the Gothic Line tour is based in Riccione, Cervia and Mestre and is in four star hotels. The price is £697 per person, based on two sharing. All tours are for seven nights.

CAMPING

Caravan & Camping Service (071-792 1944)
Lake Maggiore, Lake Garda, Tuscany and the Lido di Jesolo. For example, 14 nights on the campsite on Lake Maggiore ranges from £366 to £480 for two adults and two children. This price includes a return ferry crossing. There are additional charges for trailers and caravans which range from £10 to £40.

EuroSites (0706 830888)
Tent and mobile home holidays on Lake Garda, Lido di Jesolo and the Tuscan coast. For example, two weeks in a mobile home at the Garden Paradiso site in Lido di Jesolo costs from £269 to £1099 for a party of up to eight people inclusive of accommodation and ferry.

Eurocamp Travel Ltd (0565 626262)
Tuscany, Umbria, Campania, Italian Lakes, Dolomites, Adriatic/Venice and Trieste. Accommodation is in six berth fully equipped tents and eight berth fully equipped mobile homes. For example, 14 nights near Trieste in a tent for two adults and up to four children costs from £189 to £795. 14 nights in a mobile home for two adults and up to six children costs from £371 to £1215. Prices include a short sea ferry crossing.

Haven Europe (0705 466111)
Destinations include Lake Garda and Venice. Tents and mobile homes are offered. The sites are large and have good sporting facilities. A 14 night mobile home holiday at Cisano on Lake Garda costs from £405 to £1268 for two adults – children under 14 go free. The price includes ferry travel.

Sunsites (0565 625555)
Self-drive camping and mobile home holidays in Tuscany, Venice and Lake Garda. For example, a 12 night holiday on the Camping Union Lido site near Venice costs from £123 to £356 for two adults and two children, ferry inclusive.

Venue Holidays (0233 629950)
Destinations include the Venetian Riviera and Tuscany. A two week holiday at the Camping Marina di Venezia at Punta Sabbioni costs from £199 to £692 for a six berth tent. This price includes the cross Channel ferry from Ramsgate to Dunkirk and 12 nights at the resort for two adults and up to four children.

CARAVANS

Caravan & Camping Service (071-792 1944)
Destinations include Lake Garda and the Adriatic Coast. Campsite accommodation with pitches bookable nightly. For

example, 14 nights costs from £120 to £200 for two adults, car and caravan. Ferry travel is extra.

CITY BREAKS

A T Mays City Breaks (041 331 1121)
Rome, Florence and Venice. For example, a two night weekend break on a bed and breakfast basis at the two star Mariano Hotel in Rome costs from £274 per person, flight inclusive. The same break at the five star Bernini Bristol Hotel costs from £405 per person.

Aeroscope (0608 50103)
Short breaks to cities all over Italy featuring Best Western hotels. For example, two nights at the four star Hotel Paradiso in Naples costs from around £300 to £400 per person, on a bed and breakfast basis, flight inclusive.

Cresta Holidays (061-927 7000)
Short break holidays all over Italy. For example, a two night bed and breakfast break to Venice, staying at the two star San Zulian Hotel costs from £262 to £338 per person, flight inclusive.

Italian Escapades (081-748 2661)
Cities featured include Venice, Rome, Florence, Verona, Milan, Bologna, Naples, Pisa, Parma and Padua. Two weeks in low season at the Hotel Scalzi in Verona on bed and breakfast costs £494 per person, based on two sharing. Two weeks in high season at the Hotel Grand in Florence on a bed and breakfast basis costs £1943 per person, based on two people sharing. Prices include return charter flights.

Italiatour (071-371 1114)
Destinations include Rome, Florence, Venice, Milan, Turin and Bologna. For example, a three night trip to Milan staying at the New York Hotel on a bed and breakfast basis, costs from £290 to £358 per person, flight inclusive.

Kirker Holidays (071-231 3333)
All grades of city hotel are offered throughout Italy. The company also has a range of luxury country hotels. For

example, a three night bed and breakfast holiday in Venice, by air from London, including arrival transfer and staying at a two star hotel costs from £329 per person. A seven night bed and breakfast holiday to Florence staying in a three star hotel costs from £403 to £440 per person, flight inclusive.

Made to Measure Holidays (0243 533333)
Venice, Florence and Siena. A two night stay at the three star Hotel Caterina in Siena on a bed and breakfast basis costs from £217 to £312 per person, flight inclusive.

Magic of Italy (081-748 7575)
Destinations include Venice, Florence, Rome and Verona. Accommodation is in three, four and five star hotels including those in a 16th century tower, a 17th century building converted from a monastery, an historic building that was once a convent, a 15th century Doge's palace, a 14th century palace and an English cottage. Prices range from £610 for two people in a twin room on a bed and breakfast basis at Porta Rossa in Florence to £2783 for two people in a twin room on a bed and breakfast basis at the Hotel Cipriani in Venice. Prices include return charter flights and transfers.

Skybus Holidays (071-373 6055)
Destinations include Venice, Florence and Rome. For example, a stay at the Hotel Machiavelli in Florence costs from £33 to £45 per night. Flights to Florence cost from £129 to £179 per person for a charter flight and from £179 to £329 per person for a scheduled flight. Combinations of two, three or even four cities are offered.

Sovereign (0293 599988)
Rome, Venice and Florence. For example, a three night break at the three star Hotel Orazia in Rome, staying on a bed and breakfast basis, costs from £177 per person.

Thomson (081-200 8733)
Rome, Florence and Venice. For example, a three night bed and breakfast holiday for a family of three in Venice costs from £542.

CLUB HOLIDAYS

Club Med (071-581 1161)
Club Med have three villages on the mainland, two on the island of Sicily and two on Sardinia. For example, seven nights at the Donoratico strawhut village on the Tuscan coast between Livorno and Piombino costs from £438 to £616 per person, flight inclusive.

Mark Warner (071-938 1851)
Tyrrhenian Coast of southern Italy. A seven night full-board package at the Club Punta Licosa costs from £495 to £701 per person, including return air travel from Gatwick.

COACH HOLIDAYS

Airtours (0706 260000)
An eight day Classic Italy tour costs from £449 to £489 per person. This price includes return flights to Verona and visits to Verona, Venice, Siena, Florence and Lake Garda.

Astons Coaches (0905 821390)
Trips to the Adriatic Riviera during an eight week summer period. For example, a 14 day camping holiday costs £249 per person. This price includes all coach travel and 11 nights tent accommodation.

Contiki Travel (081-290 6422)
Coach tours for the 18-35s. For example, a guided 12 day tour which departs from and returns to Rome. Places visited include Florence, Sorrento, Assisi and Venice. Accommodation is based on triple share with private facilities. Prices range from £488 to £517 per person.

Cosmosair (061 -480 5799)
Coach express, touring and air-coach holidays. For example, a 14 night coach express holiday in Lido di Jesolo costs from £199 to £315 per person, on half-board. A 10 day touring holiday on the Italian Riviera costs from £258 to £298 per person. A 15 day air-coach holiday which visits Venice, Rome, Florence and includes a seven day stay in Sorrento costs from £548 to £598 per person.

DA Tours (0383 881700)
Destinations include the Lakes, Tuscany and Sorrento. For example, a 14 night Magic of Italy tour which visits Rome, Sorrento and Florence costs from £574 to £592 per person.

Excelsior Holidays (0202 309733)
Destinations include Lake Garda, Lake Maggiore, Tuscany, the Bay of Naples, Venice and Rome. For example, a 10 day trip to Lake Garda costs from £319 to £379 per person on a half-board basis. A 13 day trip to Sorrento costs from £579 to £599 per person on a half-board basis. A 12 day trip to Montecatini in Tuscany costs from £569 per person on half-board.

Fourwinds Holidays (0452 527656)
A Lakes and Dolomites tour based in Levico and an Italian Riviera tour based in Alassio. An eight day trip to Levico with optional excursions to Venice, Verona and Lake Garda costs from £189 per person. This price includes coach travel and five nights accommodation in a family run hotel on half-board.

Insight Holidays (0800 393 393)
Escorted touring holidays. There are two itineraries to Italy: the Best of Italy which visits Rome, Venice, Italian Lakes, Milan, Pisa, Florence, Assisi, Sorrento, Capri and the Vatican City; and a Grand Tour of Italy which visits Rome, Pompeii, Sorrento, Capri, Naples, Sicily, Alberobello, San Marino, Ravenna, Venice, Italian Lakes, Milan, Pisa, Florence, Siena and the Vatican City. The Best of Italy is a 10 day trip and costs around £560 per person. The Grand Tour lasts 16 days and costs from £995 to £1030 per person.

Italiatour (071-371 1114)
The Treasures of Sicily – an eight day tour costs from £674 to £804 per person on full-board, flight inclusive.

Premier Italy (081-390 5554)
Tours which involve flying out to Italy and then staying in one or perhaps two four star hotels. Tours include Glorious Tuscany, Shakespeare's Cities, Neapolitan Magic, Treasures of Umbria and Lakes and Gardens. An eight day Glorious Tuscany tour, including half-board accommodation, costs from £567 to £619 per person, flight inclusive.

Timescape Holidays (081-980 7244)
Lake Garda and Lido di Jesolo. Self-catering apartments, pensioni and hotels. For example, 10 days in an apartment accommodating two to six people in Lido di Jesolo costs from £89 to £149 per person, inclusive of coach travel and ferry fares. Seven days in a hotel on Lake Garda costs from £99 to £149 per person, on a half-board basis and including coach travel.

Top Deck Travel (071-373 4906)
Holidays aimed at 18 to 38 year olds. Tours of between 14 and 70 days around Europe, most of which include Italy. For example, a 14 day European highlights tour which visits Pisa, Florence, Rome and Venice costs from £560 to £599 per person. This includes hotel accommodation on a triple share basis, 13 continental breakfasts and seven evening meals and all transport and ferry crossings.

COOKING HOLIDAYS

Arblaster & Clarke Wine Tours (0730 266883)
Cookery courses in Verona for groups of eight to 16 people are offered at the villa of Dante's direct descendant (at Dante's home in exile) where local dishes are prepared and combined with the high quality wine made on the estate. Based about 10 miles outside Verona. Prices are from around £750 per person for five days.

Blackheath Wine Trails (081-463 0012)
Greve in Chianti. At Villa Zeno, the private home of Giovanna Folonari. Three or four days of instruction in Tuscan family cookery (with meals prepared in the kitchen and eaten in the dining room), a day visiting wine producers, and a grand farewell dinner in the villa. Prices on request.

Italian Cookery Weeks (081-208 0112)
Umbria and Apulia. One week courses which run from May to September. The cost is £895 per person for one week's tuition, accommodation, food, wine and return flight from London.

Tasting Italy (081-964 5839)
Destinations include Sicily, Tuscany and Piedmont. Residential

tutored courses by leading Italian chefs in English. Wine tastings and cultural excursions to historical sites, towns and markets. There are a maximum of 15 people to a course. A seven night package costs from £750 to £830 per person. This includes full-board and tuition.

CRUISES

Swan Hellenic (071-831 1515)
10 cultural cruises in the Mediterranean which have ports of call in Italy. Lectures on ornithology, botany, vulcanology and astronomy are given on board. For example, the Sailing to Byzantium cruise visits Italy, Greece and Turkey. It starts from Venice and lasts for 14 days. The price is £1580 per person.

CYCLING HOLIDAYS

Fresco Cycling (0865 310399)
Destinations include Tuscany, Umbria and Lake Bolsena. Prices per night include your chosen itinerary, accommodation, cycle hire and transfer of luggage. They range from £45 per person for accommodation in a village house to £95 per person for a stay in a Premier deluxe hotel.

Liaisons Abroad (071-384 1122)
Veneto. Accompanied cycling holidays based in Verona. Three to six night itineraries from £439 to £884 per person, including full-board accommodation, tour leader, support vehicles and cycle hire.

GARDEN TOURS

The Travel Club of Upminster (0708 225000)
Lake Orta. The Gardens of the Italian Lakes. Seven nights half-board at the Hotel Giardinetto, on Lake Orta costs £498 per person. This price includes three excursions to the gardens of the region.

GOLFING HOLIDAYS

Italian Escapades (081-748 2661)

Sardinia. A two week holiday at the Hotel Due Lune at Puntaldia costs from £1102 to £2479 per person on a half-board basis. A nine hole golf course is set along the coast, 50 yards from the hotel. Green fees are free to guests during May, June, September and October. There is a special 50% reduction per day at other times. Prices include return charter flights.

HORSERIDING

Gordon Overland (0228 26795)

Holidays in Northern Italy from around £350 per person, per week.

Sardatur Holidays (071-637 0281)

Sardinia. A seven night package with five days riding costs £698 per person, including full-board accommodation and flights.

LANGUAGE LEARNING

Euro-Academy (081-686 2363)

Florence, Rome, Siena and Milan. For example, a two week intensive course in Florence costs £250 per person. Accommodation is in private homes and costs £14 to £20 per night. Air fares are not included.

Gordon Overland (0228 26795)

Rome – throughout the year. For example, a fortnight's holiday with full-board and tuition on a one to one basis for 10 hours per week costs £600 per person, flight inclusive.

MUSIC HOLIDAYS

Arblaster & Clarke Wine Tours (0730 266883)

Trips to Verona in July and August combined with visits to vineyards in the region. The trips are escorted by Charles

Metcalfe of Wine Magazine – and a former opera singer. Prices start at £669 per person. Operas this year include Nabuco, Aida and Otello and tickets are also available for a very special one off performance by Placido Domingo in August.

Brompton Travel (081-549 3334)
Opera holidays on the Italian Lakes and Naples. For example, a stay on Lake Maggiore is combined with visits to La Scala in Milan, Turin and Genoa. A week's holiday costs approximately £1150 per person. This includes flights by scheduled service, half-board accommodation, excursions and opera tickets.

Liaisons Abroad (071-384 1122)
Opera ticket reservations for all major theatres in Italy. Prices range from £17 in Verona during the Arena Festival to £198 in Milan for the Teatro alla Scala. Accommodation can also be arranged.

Martin Randall Travel (081-742 3355)
Opera in Verona. For example, a seven day trip which includes tickets to see La Boheme, Otello, Norma and Nabucco costs £1280 per person, flight inclusive. Accommodation is in the three star Hotel Bologna which is a few yards from the Arena. Groups are small and have between 15 and 25 participants. There is a fair amount of walking on the art-historical walks and excursions.

Page & Moy (0533 524433)
Five or seven nights by air from Heathrow and Gatwick to the Verona Opera Festival. Departure dates are from July 5th to August 31st. 'The 1994 Verona Opera Festival is the 72nd to be held in the great amphitheatre. Five operas will receive the Arena treatment in 1994 – lavish spectacle and splendour for which Verona has become renowned. The repertoire is particularly challenging for it includes Bellini's seldom-performed Norma and Verdi's late masterpiece Otello.' There is a choice of hotels either on the shores of Lake Garda or in the town of Bassano del Grappa. Prices include tickets to two or three performances, half-board accommodation and flights. The cost ranges from £499 to £995 per person.

Timescape Holidays (081-980 7244)

An inclusive coach tour to Verona for seven nights staying on Lake Garda costs £289 per person. This includes tickets to the opera and return coach travel. Accommodation is on a half-board basis.

Travel for the Arts (071-483 4466)

Escorted tours to Venice, Naples, Milan, Turin and Genoa which include flights, accommodation, tickets to at least one opera, ballet or concert and guided sightseeing programmes. Prices start at around £600 per person. Tours to summer festivals in Florence, Verona, Pesaro, Macerata and Parma are also offered at around £600 per person.

Winterski/Vita Holidays (0273 626242)

Opera packages to Milan, Verona and Rome. For example, a three night trip to Verona costs from £369 to £399 per person. This price includes bed and breakfast accommodation, two opera performances and return flights.

PAINTING AND DRAWING HOLIDAYS

Artscape Painting Holidays (0702 435990)

10 day courses in Positano on the Amalfi coast and Siena in Tuscany. Prices range between £1134 and £1242 per person. The prices include half-board accommodation, return flights, excursions and tuition.

Liaisons Abroad (071-384 1122)

Art lessons and accompanied visits based in Verona. Seven night stays cost from £465 per person, including bed and breakfast accommodation, lecturer, guide and entrance fees.

Magic of Italy (081-748 7575)

A weekly painting course in Tuscany staying at Casa Elisabetta villa-apartment. It caters for painters of all levels. Prices include a return flight and car hire with unlimited mileage and cost £369 for four people in a one bedroom apartment plus £155 per person for one week's painting tuition.

Verrocchio Arts Centre (071-727 3313)
Painting and sculpture holidays in a hilltop village in Tuscany from June to September. Prices range from £337 to £520 per person for 13 nights. Prices include 11 days of tuition and include either self-catering or half-board accommodation. Air fares are not included.

Pilgrimages

Spes Travel (071-821 5144)
Trips to Rome, Assisi and Florence. For example, a seven night full-board package to Rome which includes visits to the Basilica of St Peter, the Catacombs and a conducted tour of Christian Rome costs around £520 per person, with scheduled flights from Heathrow. A seven night full-board package to Assisi costs £520 per person. Christmas in Rome, with seven nights' stay in the Casa Tra Noi Hotel on one of the hills of Rome and only a few minutes walk from St Peter's and the Vatican costs around £520 per person.

Sailing

Crestar Yacht Charters (071-730 9962)
Yachting in the Ligurian Sea, on the Amalfi Coast or in Sardinia. For example, a 70ft sailing sloop with captain, cook and steward cruising out of San Remo on tailor-made itineraries to include Portofino, Rapallo, Sestri Levante and Elba costs around £14000 per week for six people, excluding flights.

Skiing

Mark Warner (071-938 1851)
Courmayeur. A seven night half-board ski package at the Club Telecabine costs from £366 to £557 per person, including return air travel from Gatwick.

Thomson (081-200 8733)
Bormio. A 14 night self-catering holiday for a family of four

costs from £1029 to £1630 at Residence Jolly. Equipment hire, ski school and lift passes are extra.

Winterski/Vita Holidays (0273 626242)
Destinations include Lombardia, Trentino and Piemonte. For example, seven night packages to Lombardia cost from £259 to £349 per person. This price includes half-board accommodation, transfers and return flights.

MAIN ITALIAN SKI RESORTS

Bormio (4,018ft):
Those travelling here by air have a drive from Milan which can often take almost four hours. Many consider it worth the trouble: Bormio in Lombardy offers a good skiing area for intermediate level skiers – and plenty of activities for non-skiers. Children are well provided for in the resort's ski school which has a good reputation.
Operators:
Enterprise (061-745 7000); Neilson (0532 394555); Ski Thomson (021-632 6282).

Cervinia (6,724ft):
Once the favoured resort of Mussolini, in whose era Cervinia became the smart place to visit. Some would say that the place has been in decline ever since. In fact, this resort in the Aosta Valley is making a comeback and rising fast in popularity. It boasts the longest and highest piste in Italy (the Ventina which is five miles long). It is a particularly good place for beginners with plenty of nursery slopes. The nearest airport is Turin 73 miles away, about two and a half hours by car.
Operators:
Airtours (0706 260000); Crystal (081-399 5144); Enterprise (061-745 7000); Inghams (081-785 7777); Neilson (0532 394555); Ski Thomson (021-632 6282).

Cortina (4,002ft):
Unashamedly describing itself as the "Queen of the Dolomites", Cortina certainly has few challengers for its throne as the most complete winter sports resort in the whole of Italy (it hosted the Winter Olympics in 1956). It has good all round skiing and plenty of beginners' areas. Its one drawback is

rather a long transfer from Venice, about two and a half hours' drive away.
Operators:
Bladon Lines (081-785 3131); Crystal (081-399 5144).

Courmayeur (4,034ft):
If there were nothing else to recommend Courmayeur, it has the advantage of being the nearest Italian ski resort to Britain – just a brief drive from the end of the Mont Blanc tunnel in the Aosta Valley. In fact Courmayeur has a lot going for it as well as proximity: it offers around 60 miles of skiing and spectacular views of Mont Blanc. The nursery slopes are not of the best, but the ski school is satisfactory.
Operators:
Bladon Lines (081-785 3131); Crystal (081-399 5144); Enterprise (061-745 7000); Inghams (081-785 7777); Interski (0623 551024); Mark Warner (071-938 1851); Neilson (0532 394555); Ski Thomson (021-632 6282).

Livigno (5,970ft):
A spectacular airport transfer (over five hours away from Milan) might dissuade most families from considering Livigno which would be a pity. In fact it is a very good resort for children with a good choice of nursery slopes, plenty of easy runs and five separate ski schools.
Operators:
Airtours (0706 260000); Crystal (081-399 5144); Enterprise (061-745 7000); Inghams (081-785 7777); Neilson (0532 394555); Ski Thomson (021-632 6282).

Sauze d'Oulx (4,920ft):
Just 50 miles from Turin, this resort has the advantage of a relatively short airport transfer. Until recently it also had a bad reputation for attracting the Alpine equivalent of lager louts. These days life at the resort is generally more sedate.
Operators:
Airtours (0706 260000); Enterprise (061-745 7000); Ski Thomson (021-632 6282).

Selva, Val Gardena (5,084ft):
Selva is the best known resort in the Dolomites and offers a huge intermediate skiing area and excellent facilities for children

and beginners. (The other resorts in Val Garden are Santa Cristina and Oritsei). The scenery of the Val Garden is spectacular, surrounded by the massive peaks of Sella and Sassolungo.
Operators:
Bladon Lines (081-785 3131); Crystal (081-399 5144); Enterprise (061-745 7000).

La Thuile (4,756ft):
A purpose-built resort with a varied choice of skiing areas, with a particuarly good selection of intermediate runs and nursery slopes. The main skiing area is above the Petit-St-Bernard pass, the route chosen by Hannibal when he took his elephants over the Alps to attack Rome in 218BC. One of its drawbacks is a lack of things to do for non-skiers.
Operators:
Bladon Lines (081-785 3131); Crystal (081-399 5144); Enterprise (061-745 7000); Neilson (0532 394555).

SPA HOLIDAYS

Thermalia Travel (071-483 1898)
Abano Terme, Montegrotto and Montecatini. For example, seven nights in a three star hotel, including five treatments, flights and full-board costs from £579 to £699 per person.

STUDY HOLIDAYS

Gordon Overland (0228 26795)
Lombardy – tours which cover a range of subjects cost around £650 per person for 14 days, flight inclusive. These holidays are featured in Spring only.

TENNIS

Italian Escapades (081-748 2661)
Malcesine, Lake Garda. A two week holiday at the Hotel Tennis Centre Olivi ranges in price from £634 to £823 per person, on half-board and based on two people sharing a twin room. The hotel has seven tennis courts, four floodlit and some

covered. There is also a swimming pool. Special tennis weeks on full-board with free tennis are available. Prices include return charter flights.

WALKING AND TREKKING

Exodus (081-675 5550)
Accompanied walking holiday based in the Lungiana Hills, Tuscany, costs from £450 to £480 per person for 14 days. This price includes bed and breakfast accommodation, walks, visits to Lucca, Cinque Terre and the Marble Mountains and return air travel.

Explore Worldwide (0252 319448)
Walking through Tuscany. 15 days camping in the medieval hill towns and vineyards around Volterra, Siena and Florence. The walking is easy to moderate, the group size is approximately 12 to 16 and all baggage is transported. Prices range from £568 to £619 per person, flight inclusive.

Gordon Overland (0228 26795)
Holidays in Northern Italy from £350 per person, per week.

HF Walking Holidays (081-905 9558)
Sorrento, Tuscany and Lake Garda. A 14 night half-board package to Sorrento, for example, which includes led walks and en-suite accommodation at the three star Hotel Minerva costs from £549 per person, flight inclusive.

Inntravel (0439 71111)
The Italian Sudtirol. An independent seven night walking holiday from hotel to hotel through meadows and into the Dolomites. Baggage is transported. Accommodation is in three and four star hotels, some with swimming pools. Prices range from £558 to £695 per person, including air travel to Verona.

Ramblers Holidays (0707 331133)
All accompanied walking or sightseeing/walking parties. Destinations include Lake Garda, Sorrento Peninsula, mountains of Tuscany, Rome, Siena, Florence, Urbino and Assisi, Sicily and the hills near Padua. The hotel accommodation is

usually two star, sometimes three. All holidays are on a half-board basis. For example, one week's walking in the mountains north-east of Milan costs £369 per person, based on two sharing.

Sardatur Holidays (071-637 0281)
Sardinia. A seven night package which includes flights, full-board accommodation and walking with a guide costs £549 per person.

Sherpa Expeditions (081-577 2717)
Destinations include Tuscany and the Dolomites. Accommodation is either in hotels or camping. Continuous walking holidays are also offered in which you stay in a different hotel each night. For example, a two week walking holiday with campsite accommodation costs £649 per person. This price includes the services of a tour leader and vehicle support, air travel is also included. A one week holiday with hotel accommodation costs £595 per person, flight inclusive.

Waymark Holidays (0753 516477)
Destinations include Amalfi, the Dolomites, Tuscany and Sardinia. For example, a seven night holiday to Amalfi on a Grade one/two tour with some sightseeing costs around £515 per person. This price includes half-board accommodation and air travel.

Winterski/Vita Holidays (0273 626242)
Accompanied walking holidays to Trentino. For example, a seven night package on half-board costs from £419 per person, flight inclusive.

WINE TOURS

Arblaster & Clarke Wine Tours (0730 266883)
Tours of the wine regions. For example, a trip to Tuscany – for Chianti, Brunello and Vino Nobile, visiting Siena and Florence costs from £699 per person. This trip is accompanied by David Gleave MW of Winecellars and is for five days. It includes staying three nights in a typical Tuscan villa and one night in Florence and lunches with leading wine makers in their own

homes and castellos. A five day tour of Umbria for wine and truffles during the Truffle Fair in Gubbio in October which includes cookery demonstrations costs £849 per person. Accommodation is in a four star hotel. A trip to The Veneto for wine tasting and opera costs from £799 to £849 per person and includes wine visits and optional tickets to Aida in the Roman Amphitheatre.

Blackheath Wine Trails (081-463 0012)
Tuscany, the Veneto and Trentino. For example, a six day trip to Tuscany in Spring and Autumn, staying at the four star Plaza Hotel Lucchesi with excursions into the Tuscan countryside for tastings with producers and delightful regional meals and visiting Siena, Pisa, San Gimignano and the Chianti Classico region costs £695 per person, flights inclusive. Six days in Spring and Autumn at four star hotels in the Veneto and Trentino with wine excursions etc costs £680 per person, including flights.

Martin Randall Travel (081-742 3355)
An itinerary that combines wine tasting with art. The tour is based in Siena and included on the tour are many of the region's finest works of art. Visits to small, traditional family-run establishments will be contrasted with the 'high tech' methods of the large wine producers. The eight day trip costs £990 per person, flight inclusive. Accommodation is at the four star Hotel Athena in Siena and is on a half-board basis.

Page & Moy (0533 524433)
Seven nights by air from Heathrow or Gatwick to the Veneto, staying in the four star Hotel Belvedere in Bassano del Grappa in the foothills of the Alps. Accommodation is on a half-board basis. Excursions to the Montello hills and the White Wine Road, the Colli Euganei region, Soave, Verona and Bardolino are included. Prices range from £579 to £595 per person.

7

HOLIDAY ITALY

When most people think of a holiday in Italy, they tend to have a few pre-conceived images of the country. They think of the cities: Rome, Florence and Venice. They may think of the historical sites: the Colosseum, the Uffizi Gallery in Florence, the Leaning Tower of Pisa, the excavated city of Pompeii. And possibly they may have in mind the countryside of Tuscany. And winter sports enthusiasts will be familiar with the attractions of the country's ski resorts. Certainly all of these number among Italy's key holiday attractions – but there is more, much more to attract the tourists. Names of regions like Umbria, the Abruzzi, Apulia and Calabria are slowly beginning to establish themselves as holiday destinations and will probably soon rival the likes of Tuscany and Liguria.

Before committing yourself to a specific destination, spend some time familiarising yourself with the Complete Holiday Italy.

THE NORTH

LIGURIA

This stretch of Italian coastline is better known as the Italian Riviera – not as famous perhaps as its better known next door neighbour the French Riviera, it is nevertheless in many respects every bit as attractive. And the Italian Riviera is more suitable for family holidays. While the French Riviera consists of a series of fashionable, expensive resorts appealing to the smart set, its Italian neighbour is much more down to earth with an appealing collection of unpretentious towns. The Italian Riviera divides neatly into two with Genoa at its centre: the eastern half is known as the Riviera di Levante (of the rising sun) with the western end called the Riviera di Ponente (of the setting sun).

The best known resort of the Italian Riviera – and arguably its best resort overall – is Alassio. It is a classic, busy Italian resort with plenty of energy and ambience and a good long beach. There are plenty of other seaside places along the coast worth a look including Finale Ligure on the Riviera di Ponente and, on the Rivieria di Levante, the ultra chic Portofino and nearby Rapallo.

Genoa may not deserve a place in the first rank of Italian cities but it's worth a look for its interesting collection of *palazzos*, *gallerias* and intriguing narrow streets.

The most scenic part of Liguria is Cinque Terre – 'Five Lands' – five magnificent fishing villages situated in a breath-taking stretch of coastline. You can drive to them but it's a taxing journey by car – better to visit the Cinque Terre by boat from Sestri Levante or Portovenere, or take the train which travels through long tunnels blasted through the rock. A £2 ticket will allow you to visit all five villages comfortably in one day.

PIEDMONT

Piedmont means literally 'at the foot of the mountains' – and what mountains! Italy's north-west border can serve up glimpses of the likes of Mont Blanc and the Matterhorn. The region also features the contrasting carpet-flat plain east of Turin.

If you are driving to Italy from Britain, you will more than likely pass through Piedmont. If you have the time, break your journey at Turin. The city is well-known as the home of the Fiat factory (famously featured along with the rest of Turin in the Michael Caine film *The Italian Job*). As it is an automobile producer you might have assumed that Turin was grim and industrial – in fact it is one of the most attractive cities in Italy.

As the home of the old House of Savoy – and the place where the first King of Italy reigned – Turin is appropriately supplied with plenty of Baroque palaces, and a surfeit of hand-some churches. Turin has an excellent Egyptian museum which ranks third in the world after those of London and Cairo. And, as you might expect of a city so closely linked with the motor car, there is also an automobile museum whose exhibits include the Isotta Franchini driven by Gloria Swanson in the film Sunset Boulevard.

In the eastern Piedmont is Asti, the region which gives its

name to Italy's best known sparkling wine, the Asti Spumante. Near to the French border are Piedmont's purpose-built ski resorts including Bardonecchia, Sauze D'Oulx and Sestriere. In the northern part of the region lies the resort of Domodossola.

AOSTA VALLEY

For motorists driving into Italy through the Mont Blanc tunnel, this stunningly attractive valley will provide the first glimpse of the country. The mountains – among Europe's tallest – are breathtaking: Mont Blanc, the Matterhorn and Monte Rosa to the north and the Gran Paradiso to the south.

Aosta itself is an attractive old town with some well preserved Roman buildings. The star attraction however is Italy's second biggest national park: the Gran Paradiso, once the site of a royal hunting ground, which has a rich variety of wildlife including chamois, marmots, royal eagles, polecats and ibex.

Courmayeur is probably the best known of Italy's ski resorts: it is certainly the most stylish. The scenery, with its views of Mont Blanc, is hard to beat. Expert skiers however will probably not be daunted by the difficulty of the runs.

LOMBARDY AND THE LAKES

The Italian Lakes enjoyed a boom in popularity at about the same time as Britain's own Lake District. The likes of Wordsworth, Shelley and Byron – not to mention Queen Victoria – enjoyed the glorious contrasts in scenery offered by the Italian lakes. The British developed a particular appetite for the glorious warm summers of Maggiore, Como and Garda, relishing the chance to make the occasional foray up the snow-capped Alpine peaks which flank the lakes. Before the Second World War any British tourist visiting Italy would more than likely have been headed for Lake Como or Lake Garda rather than the Italian coastal resorts. The Lakes slipped out of fashion for a while but now they are being rediscovered by a new generation of enthusiasts. Surprisingly while all the lakes are in a relatively small area, they each have quite a different style and character.

Lake Maggiore is very long – 40 miles from end to end: the top end lies in Switzerland – and narrow (no more than three miles wide at its widest point). The lakeside towns are pleasant enough, particularly Stresa, Pallanza and Cannero but Maggiore's greatest delight are the Borromean Islands, the dots of land that lie a boat ride from Stresa. Isola Madre, Isola Pescatori and Isola Bella each have their attractions – but if you have time to see only one, opt for Isola Bella with its handsome palace and carefully sculpted gardens.

To the west of Maggiore is Lake Orta, which is a complete contrast to its bigger neighbour: small, intimate and timeless. The old town of Orta, where cars are prohibited, is a delight – full of interesting shops and good restaurants.

To the east of Maggiore, Lake Lugano is largely in Switzerland and its scenery is distinctly more rugged. The Italian part most worth visiting is Campione, an Italian enclave.

The best known of the lakes is probably Lake Como, which in terms of scenery and ambience offers the most variety. People may argue about whether it is the prettiest of the lakes, however it is certainly the deepest of them, reaching a depth of 1,345ft – making it the deepest in Europe. Its main resorts include Bellagio, Menaggio, Cernobbio and Como. Its principal sights number the Villa Carlotta with its magnificent gardens; the Gardens of the Villa Monastero; and Comacina Island.

The largest of the lakes – and the largest lake in Italy – is Lake Garda which is over 30 miles long and is 11 miles wide at its widest point. In many places, with its pebbly beach, you can easily imagine you were beside a sea rather than on a lake. Its favoured climate encourages a huge variety of plants: on the shores you can see, for example, the Bardolino vines, lemon trees and masses of oleanders and cypress trees.

The least known of all the lakes is Lake Iseo which is just over 15 miles long. Pretty in parts, downright ugly in others, it is clear why it is less visited than its bigger, prettier neighbours.

The main city of Lombardy is Milan, Italy's financial capital (see Chapter 9). Its most famous tourist attraction is Leonardo da Vinci's painting of the Last Supper which can be seen in the Church of Santa Maria delle Grazie. The other major shrines in the city are the marvellous marble cathedral; La Scala opera house; and the wonderfully revamped San Siro football stadium, home to both AC and Inter Milan.

Other principal cities of Lombardy worth a visit include Pavia, Bergamo, Brescia and Mantua.

Stresa: A Farewell to Arms

Ernest Hemingway first came to Stresa in September 1918. The elegant resort on the shores of Lake Maggiore has a glorious setting, surrounded on two sides by the high Alps. The young Hemingway, then aged 19 and little travelled beyond the American mid-West, was entranced. The pleasures of a stay at the Grand Hotel were particularly sweet because Hemingway was in Stresa on convalescent leave. Two months previously on the Italian front near Treviso he had come close to death when a trench mortar fired from the Austrian lines landed in a dug-out which he was sharing with some Italian soldiers.

Early in 1918 the 18-year old Hemingway had left his job as a reporter on the *Kansas City Star* and enrolled in the Italian Red Cross as an ambulance driver. Like most things to do with Hemingway's life, the exact reasons for his decision to join the Italian Red Cross are disputed – the most likely explanation is that he believed he wouldn't be accepted in the US Army because of his poor eyesight. In June he passed through Milan en route to the Red Cross centre in Schio near the Austrian front in north-east Italy. After a failed offensive, the Austrians had dug in along the River Piave. It was near Fossalta di Piave that Hemingway was injured while delivering cigarettes and chocolate to soldiers in the front lines. The trench mortar explosion which killed one of the Italian soldiers in the dug-out and badly injured the two others, left Hemingway with 227 separate wounds in his legs which required further difficult operations to remove the mortar fragments and a lengthy convalescence.

Hemingway's injuries earned him the Italian Silver Medal for valour. He also won temporary celebrity as the first American to be wounded in the Italian campaign. He was rapidly transferred to the Red Cross Hospital in Milan where he met the first great love of his life.

The fascinating thing about Hemingway is that the real events of his life tend to be more interesting than his books. In the best of his books, Hemingway's real life and his fiction are often spun together in a single thread. *A Farewell to Arms* published in 1928, perhaps provides the most successful mix of fact and fancy – and is arguably his greatest literary work.

Frederic Henry, the hero of the book, is indistinguishable from Hemingway. Like the young writer he is a Red Cross ambulance driver on the Piave front – and Henry receives a

trench mortar wound identical to Hemingway's (the fiction-
alised version of the incident is said to be the most accurate
account of Hemingway's real injury). And Henry, like
Hemingway, ends up at the Red Cross hospital in Milan where
he too falls in love with a nurse. But here fact and fantasy separate: Hemingway's love affair with the nurse Agnes von
Kurowsky was probably platonic and the romance was relatively short-lived. The fictional relationship as written by
Hemingway was quite different. Frederic Henry and his
English nurse Catherine Barkley embark on a romance steamy
enough to get *Scribner's* magazine – which was carrying instal-
ments of the book – banned from news-stands in Boston.

Hemingway spent his 10 day convalescent leave in Stresa
separated from Agnes (after seven days he rushed back to
Milan to be with her), and had plenty of time to yearn for the
sort of passionate affair enjoyed by his fictional alter-ego. But
the only sport he enjoyed at the hotel was a regular game of
billiards with another guest, 99-year old Count Greppi (who
would appear in *A Farewell to Arms* as Count Greffi).
Hemingway filled his days by rowing on the lake and one day
taking a trip to the top of the Mottarone to enjoy its stunning
view over the seven Italian lakes. 'This beats paradise all to
hell,' he observed at the time.

Seventy-five years on, Stresa can still legitimately challenge
paradise as a holiday destination. Stresa's Grand Hotel des Iles
Borromees is that rare sort of five-star place: smart and stylish
but nevertheless thoroughly welcoming. The man at the desk
was happy to show me the rooms taken by Hemingway when
he returned to the hotel in 1948. Did he know which room
Hemingway took when he originally came in 1918? 'I think it
was the same one,' he said. But it seems unlikely that a conva-
lescing Red Cross lieutenant would have been furnished with
the grand rooms that now make up the Presidential suite in
numbers 105 and 106. But being Hemingway, it would not be
surprising if he had managed to talk his way into the best
room in the house.

In the novel, Frederic Henry takes 'a good room': 'It was
very big and light and looked out on the lake. The clouds were
down over the lake but it would be beautiful with the
sunlight.' The man from the desk flung open the shutters and
revealed a glorious view. On this morning there were no
clouds and indeed the lake *was* beautiful.

Later in the novel, Hemingway writes: 'I remember waking in the morning. Catherine was asleep and the sunlight was coming in through the window. The rain had stopped and I stepped out of bed and across the floor to the window. Down below were the gardens, bare now but beautifully regular, the gravel paths, the trees, the stone wall by the lake and the lake in the sunlight with the mountains beyond.'

The desk man and I stepped out on to the wide terrace, and it was all as Hemingway had described. The desk man pointed towards the snow-capped mountains at the far end of Lake Maggiore: 'There is Switzerland: round the corner Locarno.' He pointed to the islands in the foreground: 'The Borromean islands: Isola Bella, Isola Pescatori and Isola Madre, very pretty – you must take the boat and visit.' (In the book Henry rows to Isola Pescatori – the fisherman's island. I took the regular boat service from the Stresa landing stage to Bella and Pescatori and found them both delightful: serene and charming – and all patrolled by armies of yowling cats.)

I looked around the bedroom. On each side of the double bed little thin towels like bath mats were laid so that guests getting up did not have to touch the carpet with their bare feet. In the bathroom neatly wrapped towelling robes waited to be worn (these can be purchased from reception, said a notice on them – just in case any departing visitor felt the urge to pop one in his bag). 'Much of this furniture is the same that would have been here when Hemingway came. Except the television. And the mini-bar, of course.' Hemingway would no doubt have greatly appreciated the contents of the mini-bar.

I returned to the cocktail bar to keep the pianist company. Like Frederic Henry I ordered a dry martini. In *A Farewell to Arms* Hemingway describes the hotel barman's dry martinis as 'cool and clean'. To me, unfamiliar with the lethal mixture of gin and bitters, the martini tasted more like high octane rocket fuel.

In the book the hotel's barman proves to be Henry's saviour, providing him with the rowing boat in which he escapes with Catherine Barkley across the lake to Switzerland, evading capture by the Italian authorities and finally running away from the war. 'People ask me if I know who the character of the barman was based on,' said the manager. Pointing to the present barman, he said: 'I tell them it was his grandfather.' Is this true? 'They are satisfied when I tell them this.' What did the manager think of *A Farewell to Arms*? 'I've never read the book. I must do so one day.'

TRENTINO AND ALTO ADIGE

This is a region with a split personality. Alto-Aldige in the north, on the border between Austria and Italy, is more Austrian in character than Italian. It came into Italian possession after the end of the First World War (a fact much resented by many of the locals of Austrian descent). Trentino on the other hand is predominantly Italian and was an unwilling part of the Austro-Hungarian empire for almost 100 years – and was grateful to be returned to Italian control after the First World War.

The area's great attraction is the beautiful scenery of the Dolomites which offer skiing holidays in the winter (its best known resort is Cortina d'Ampezzo which describes itself as the "Queen of the Dolomites"). The area also has plenty of well-marked trails offering good walking in the summer. There are four long-distance footpaths (Alta Via) in the Dolomites which can take up to two weeks to complete

Principal towns include Bolzano, the capital of the Alto Adige and Trento, which lies on the road to the Brenner Pass to Austria. The most attractive town in the region is Merano which lies at the end of the Val Venosta in the Adige Valley.

FRULI-VENEZIA GIULIA

This region at the north-eastern edge of Italy combines a mixture of mountains, plains and beaches. The geographic diversity is matched by a complex ethnic mix of Slavs and German minorities. Its best-known city is Trieste, the largest port on the Adriatic, which only came under full Italian control in 1954 after a plebiscite and much debate. The city has an interesting historic centre but there is little to attract the holidaymaker.

Aquileia was a flourishing market town in Roman days. It has some interesting ruins and an archaeological museum. Udine, the capital of the region, is an attractive town once under the control of the Venetian republic. The Adriatic coastline has several resorts and a number of good beaches, particularly popular with holidaymakers from Germany and Austria.

VENETO

This region, which includes the cities of Venice, Verona, Vicenza and Padua within its borders, ranks second only to Tuscany in its attractiveness to the British holidaymaker.

While most visitors will undoubtedly put Venice at the top of their list (see Chapter 9 for a guide to the city), the other cities are as attractive in their own ways. Vicenza, for example, is the home of Palladio – the last great architect of the Renaissance. One of Palladio's finest buildings the Basilica can be seen in the city's Piazza dei Signori. The Corso Andrea Palladio, Vicenza's main street, features palaces designed by the architect and his pupils.

Padua is another fine old historic city with a magnificent array of buildings. The city's university founded in 1222, once, had Galileo as a professor. The perfectly preserved 16th century anatomy theatre, the oldest in Europe, is worth a visit. The most famous sight is probably Giotto's fresco cycle which can be viewed in the Scrovegni Chapel.

In its allure to the tourist, Verona ranks second only to Venice. Many come for its celebrated festival of opera staged every year in the arena, the Roman amphitheatre which dominates the city centre and is one of the biggest amphitheatres in the world – in Roman times it was able to accommodate up to 25,000 people.

Just as many visitors – particularly Japanese visitors – come to Verona because it was here that William Shakespeare set the play *Romeo and Juliet*. You can see (free of charge) Juliet's balcony near the Piazza delle Erbe, you can also pay to see Juliet's tomb. This may be tourism based on showbusiness rather than history, but who cares?

The Veneto is good touring country: as well as the major cities, there is also plenty of attractive countryside and many pleasant smaller towns such as Treviso with its arcaded streets and designer-label shops.

The main seaside places are Lido di Jesolo, about an hour's drive from Venice, which has a long beach but which is now beginning to look a little tarnished. The Venice Lido can also boast a long beach – it also has some of the most expensive hotels in Europe, including the well-known Cipriani.

EMILIA ROMAGNA

This is the heartland of northern Italy: a region, lying between Lombardy and Tuscany, that stretches from the Adriatic almost to the Mediterranean. As well as some of Italy's most popular seaside places, it also includes a number of its most attractive historic cities.

The holidaymaker is most likely to be drawn to the region by Rimini, the best known of Italy's resorts. It has a faithful following among Italian families who return summer after summer to enjoy its well-ordered attractions which include a good beach and plenty of nightlife. While it is big and brassy, it is certainly no Benidorm: while there are plenty of British and German tourists in evidence during the summer peak, Rimini is still very much an Italian place.

Tougher pollution controls have happily seen dramatic improvements in Rimini's sea water which was affected during the mid-1980s by an algae that became known in the British tabloids as the "killer seaweed".

The favourite excursion for Rimini holidaymakers is a day-trip to San Marino, the world's smallest republic (and tormentors of the England football team in their hapless World Cup campaign). San Marino's greatest attraction, however, is not its football team but its duty-free shops.

Emilia Romagna's historic cities are a fascinating collection. Bologna, best known for giving its name to a spaghetti sauce, is a handsome university city with delightful arcaded streets and a skyline bristling with towers and campaniles (and it has a couple of leaning towers of its own!).

Parma (a name forever associated in the mind with ham and Parmesan cheese) is a comfortable, affluent city, which despite being badly damaged in the last war is an attractive place. It has plenty of interesting streets, lots of good restaurants and an opera house which is reckoned to have one of the most critical audiences in the whole of Italy.

Ravenna may not be so well known today, but 1500 years ago it was the capital of the Western Roman Empire and in the middle ages it was one of the key cities of Europe – the site of Rome's biggest Adriatic naval base. It is a pleasant city with interesting churches and some delightful Byzantine mosaics.

Other cities worth a look include Piacenza, which has a fine town hall and an impressive cathedral; Modena which also has an imposing cathedral and the Palazzo dei Musei with a unique collection of paintings and manuscripts; and Ferrara which was one of the marvels of Renaissance town planning.

THE CENTRE

TUSCANY

For the first-time visitor to Italy and certainly for a family holiday, it would be hard to better Tuscany. It's a surprisingly compact area – no bigger than Wales – but it offers a lot. It has among the best of the historic cities with Florence and Siena. It has the Leaning Tower of Pisa, the wonderful old towers of San Gimignano and the fantastic hill-top town of Volterra. The countryside is sublime: delightful villages in gentle hills dotted with cypress trees.

Its principal attraction as a family holiday place is the wealth of self-catering accommodation available. Much of this is concentrated in the area known as "Chianti-shire" north of Siena and south of Florence. The most attractive part of Chianti is to the west of the busy motorway that links Siena and Florence.

Florence, unlike other historic cities with a big reputation, really does live up to your expectations. The art galleries are stunning: the Uffizi Gallery is worth the queue for a look at Botticelli's *Birth of Venus* and the other masterpieces of Renaissance art. You will also want to see Michelangelo's famous sculpture of David in the Accademia. You could spend several days just in the art galleries and museums.

But there is more to the city than art. The Duomo and churches like Santa Croce are magnificent. If you have children in tow, you will probably be happy to confine yourself to wandering the streets, sampling the fare of its many excellent eating places and dipping into the extraordinary array of shops.

Thankfully Siena is on the whole much more relaxed than Florence but it is every bit as fascinating. The narrow streets offer welcome shade from the heat of a summer's day. In the Piazza del Campo, where on 2 July and 16 August every year the famous Palio horse race is run, tables and chairs spill out from bars offering somewhere quiet to sip a beer and watch the world go by. Other Tuscan places worth a visit include San Gimignano, Volterra, Lucca, Pisa (if only for the Leaning Tower), Montepulciano, Montalcino and Monteriggioni.

Tuscany's one major disappointment is its lack of a good seaside place. There are a crop of beach resorts located between Carrara and Viareggio – the Riviera della Versilia – but none of them are outstanding. The coastline tends to be over-developed and over-priced; any ambience is ruined by the close proximity of the motorway and railway line. Unlike Rimini on the Adriatic where much has been done to clean up the sea, here the sea water remains polluted.

Florence: A Room With a View

The Jennings Riccioli is an agreeable three star Florentine hotel on the right bank of the River Arno, a short walk from the Ponte Vecchio. The best evidence suggests that this modest hotel – or at least this hotel in a previous guise – provided the model for the Pension Bertolini in E M Forster's novel *A Room with a View*.

When I walk up to the desk, the smartly dressed receptionist shrugs his shoulders and turns his hands palm downwards. *'Me dispiace* – tonight we are full.' I explain that my interest is not in a room but a view; I show him my Penguin Classics edition.

'Fooster!' he cries with delight. 'A M Fooster: si, si – this is the hotel. Perhaps you would like to see the room?'

This is possible?

'Yes, but of course.' He rings a bell and summons the elderly housekeeper, also neatly dressed in her starched pinafore dress. 'Room 21,' he tells her in Italian, adding: 'open the windows and let them see the view.' We travel up in an arthritic lift. In Room 21, the bed is unmade, the floor littered with German guides to the Uffizi and scattered pairs of training shoes. Was this the room that Forster imagined to be 'romantic' some 80 years ago? The housekeeper mimes her horror at the disorder.

She opens the windows, throws back the shutters – and there is the view.

'It was pleasant to fling wide the windows, pinching the fingers in unfamiliar fastenings, to lean out into sunshine with beautiful hills and trees and marble churches opposite, and, close below, the Arno, gurgling against the embankment of the road.' [*Chapter 2, A Room with a View*]

Lucy Honeychurch, the young heroine, enjoys this view – probably little changed now since Foster's day – through the generosity of fellow guests Mr Emerson and his son George. The Emersons set no store by 'views': the only serious travellers in the Bertolini party, their concern is to dip beneath the surface of 'sights' and to try and touch the heart and soul of Italy. For Forster, Italy was not so much a country, more a state of mind – agreeably at odds with the stultefying Victorianism of England. ('*One doesn't come to Italy for niceness,*' says a character in the novel: '*one comes for life.*')

This earlier part of the novel is a gentle satire on what Forster saw as the shallowness of much of the tourism to Italy at the beginning of the century. Travelling armies of Cooks' tourists, even then out to 'do' Italy. Speaking no doubt for Forster himself, the older Mr Emerson gently mocks Lucy's anguish shortly after she acquires the room with a view: through the discourtesy of Miss Lavish, she finds herself in Santa Croce church alone, without the help of her Baedeker guide book – the bible of the British abroad. The church had frescoes by Giotto '*in the presence of whose tactile values she was capable of feeling what was proper. But who was to tell her which they were?* – and which were the '*sepulchral slabs*' most praised by Ruskin? Tears of indignation prick Lucy's eyes as she realises she will be unable to pick out these sights recommended by Baedeker.

'*Then the pernicious charm of Italy worked on her, and instead of acquiring information, she began to be happy.*' Mr Emerson helps to show Lucy that Santa Croce can be enjoyed for itself rather than through the advice of her Baedeker.

Today Santa Croce is still packed with tourists, each armed with a guidebook – all looking for the recommended sights but, one fears, few seeing anything they consider memorable. For most, Santa Croce is but the latest stop on a cultural tour that is sweeping them through Italy – perhaps across Europe.

Forster's Church of England minister in Florence, the Reverend Cuthbert Eager observed the phenomenon which has now become all too familiar:

'. . . *we residents sometimes pity you poor tourists not a little – handed about like a parcel of goods from Venice to Florence, from Florence to Rome, living herded together in pensions or hotels, quite unconscious of anything that is outside Baedeker, their one anxiety to get "done" or "through" and go on somewhere else. The result is, they mix up towns, rivers, palaces in one inextricable whirl. You know the American girl in Punch who says: "Say, poppa, what did we see at Rome?" And the father replies: "Why, guess Rome was the place where we saw the yaller dog." There's travelling for you. Ha! ha! ha!'*

Today's tourists to Florence, armed with their Green Michelins and Blue Guides – perhaps the modern equivalent of the Baedeker – will find that things have changed little for the better: rather that they have got much, much worse.

Even in relatively quiet April weeks, the streets of Florence are choked by tourists, each one anxious to see all the sights. A half-hour for the Duomo, 15 minutes for the Pitti Palace. Their paths inevitably coincide at the main square, the Piazza della Signoria – for here begins the queue for the Uffizi Gallery, one of the world's greatest stores of Renaissance art treasures.

By 9am, the queue is already two or three hundred tourists long, with people who have been here waiting an hour or more to be sure of early admission. As the day goes on, the queue stretches longer and longer. Elderly couples from Philadelphia, middle aged ladies from Australia, young Parisians arm in arm, school parties laughing and pushing as they wait. Wait for what? Most seem uncertain: it's a sight, it has to be seen. An American girl, today's Lucy Honeychurch, flicks through her *Dollarwise Guide to Italy* in search of the recommended paintings: 'Botticelli – was he French or Italian?' she muses to her friend: 'Gee, so many foreign names.'

And such a long wait. The queue straggles away across the square: some can't be bothered to wait and try to push in at the Uffizi steps. An Italian boy with his girlfriend shoves in shamelessly, smiling brightly at his impudence. Three French girls steal in with cunning, they grin to each other at what they suppose to be their cleverness. An elderly man shouts at these *derniers arrives*, waving his arms with anger. The British and the Americans say nothing but complain to each other in low voices. It isn't fair, we agree: not cricket, says somebody.

Once inside, so many paintings. At the end of an hour or two of shuffling forward in the queue, the Gallery itself seems curiously irrelevant. The crowd streams on from room to room with bland indifference: those were the Botticellis, weren't those the Leonardos, get through and get out. Cross another place off the list. At the exit, two elderly Americans are grappling with the door, hoping to gain admission through an opening clearly marked "way out" in four languages. *'Sortie,'* they bark to each other: 'What's sortie: we want to get in.' The guard abruptly points them back towards the queue. 'That's the line for the gallery?' They wilt at the sight of so much patient endeavour in the cause of culture. 'Forget the gallery, honey,' says the wife, 'let's shop instead.'

Something will have to be done in Florence to control the tourists. *'Oh, the Britisher abroad!'* complains Forster's Miss Lavish: *'It's very naughty of me, but I would like to set an examination paper at Dover, and turn back every tourist who couldn't pass it.'* It's an idea.

One way to escape the Florence crowds for an afternoon is to go, like Forster's Pension Bertolini party, up the northern slopes to the nearby hilltop town of Fiesole with its handsome, opulent villas. Even now you can trace the party's route along the small road to Settignano. It's amusing to guess where amongst the olive trees they climbed down from their carriages to enjoy a sumptuous view of Florence and the Val d'Arno. And to remember that here amongst the violets, Lucy was kissed by George Emerson.

But for anyone planning to visit Tuscany during the summer, the short answer is to avoid the main cities of Florence and Siena altogether. If you really want to see them – like visiting Venice and Rome – it is probably best to go off-season, from November to March. In Tuscany, thankfully the crowds have yet to move much out of the cities.

The handsome towered city of San Gimignano – the setting for much of E M Forster's first novel *Where Angels Fear to Tread* – is the main out-of-town target for the coach parties. On market day, the narrow streets are jammed with tourists streaming in, while farmers and locals battle to make progress in the opposite direction.

Happily, beyond the cities most of Tuscany has so far been spared by these New Barbarians. Even San Gimignano is small enough and accessible enough for the overcrowding to be bearable.

Within an hour of both Florence and Siena are more than a dozen small towns, as historic, charming and fascinating as these two major cities. Places like the old town of Volterra with its marvellous Etruscan museum, the old quarter of Colle di Val d'Elsa, wholly unspoilt Casole d'Elsa, Mensano and Radicondoli. You will certainly find tourists in these places –

most of the old country farmhouses seem to be owned by Germans or Swiss – but there are never enough incomers to affect the atmosphere or pace of life. The locals will unfailingly greet you with a polite *buongiorno* or *buona sera*.

This latest invasion of tourists, like the many previous invasions which have swept through this land, is observed with polite detachment. The invaders come and eventually they go: and life goes on. When the sun shines, the Chianti is good and the pasta is fresh and gently cooked *al dente*, all other worries pale into insignificance.

Sunday night in a village bar: a warm evening beneath a sky bright with stars. Football on the television, a glass of chilled red wine, a bowl of pistachio nuts: 'And even the ranks of Tuscany could scarce forbear to cheer . . .'

THE MARCHES

Lying on the Adriatic side of the Appenine Mountains, the Marches has not received the attention – nor the volume of tourists – which are visited upon neighbouring Tuscany or Umbria. The Marches name derives from the fact that the lands which once made up the region were the frontier provinces of the Frankish Empire and the papal domains.

While it has its ration of historic towns, most British holiday-makers are likely to come here for its coastline. The best seaside resort is undoubtedly Pesaro, an attractive old city with a good beach. Fano, a short drive down the coast from Pesaro, also has some good beaches and an interesting town centre.

Ancona, the chief town of the Marches, is built in the form of an amphitheatre on the slopes of a rocky promontory. It was badly damaged in the war and has little to attract holiday-makers. However the road which runs along the coast south of Ancona – the Riviera del Conero – provides a very attractive drive.

Inland, the old city of Urbino should be visited if only for a look at its glorious Ducal Palace reckoned by many to be one of the finest works of Renaissance architecture. The National Gallery of the Marches in the city has paintings by Piero della Francesca and Raphael. The views from the city, built on two hills, are spectacular.

UMBRIA

In terms of scenic good looks, Umbria has everything that its next-door neighbour Tuscany can boast: rolling wooded hills, peaceful forests and sweet valleys (it refers to itself unashamedly as 'the green heart of Italy'). But while Tuscany has a bevy of world-class cities to attract the tourist such as Florence, Siena and Pisa – Umbria's single draw is Assisi.

The region is the birthplace of a number of saints, including St Benedict and St Rita, but its most famous saint is unquestionably St Francis. His name is forever linked with Assisi a small hilltop town with its huge, sprawling Basilica di San Francesco dedicated to the memory of St Francis.

The capital of Umbria is Perugia, a city which doesn't impress at first glance. The suburbs are sprawling, modern and industrial; the medieval centre reached after a steep climb (once you have found somewhere to park the car) seems gloomy. The place however grows on you. The views, for example, over the valley below are simply stunning. And unlike some old Italian cities, which don't seem lived in, Perugia is a lively university town with plenty of life, particularly in the evening.

Other recommended places include Gubbio, Spoleto, Orvieto (well known for its white wine) and Montefalco.

LAZIO

The principal attraction of the Lazio region is, of course, Rome which inevitably dominates the surrounding countryside. But once you have explored Rome (see Chapter 9), there are still a number of worthwhile sights outside the city. There are also several seaside resorts, the ones closest to the Italian capital can become very crowded in the season – the places on the coast south of Anzio are the best prospects.

The island of Ponza, reached by ferries from Anzio, Terracina and Formia, is the largest of the Pontine islands and one of the most attractive seaside places within striking distance of Rome.

The principal historic sights, Ostia Antica and Hadrian's villa at Tivoli, can be accommodated in a day trip or half-day trip from the capital. In the north of the region Tarquinia and Viterbo are the two main places of interest. Romans escaping the city at weekends often head for lakes Bracciano, Vico and Bolsena.

ABRUZZI

It is not surprising that few tourists visit the Abruzzi. It has few of the historical or artistic treasures of the regions to the north. Its principal attraction is its mountainous terrain, especially the Gran Sasso d'Italia mountain range and, in particular, the Corno Grande – at 2914m the highest mountain in the Apennines. It is said that bears and wolves can still be seen in the Abruzzo National Park.

The main town of the region is L'Aquila, a delightful place which because of the surrounding mountains enjoys pleasantly cool temperatures in summer. It has an interesting castle and a good collection of medieval art, but most visitors who come to L'Aquila stay here because it offers a good base for exploring the mountains of the Gran Sasso.

Sulmona, the birthplace of the poet Ovid, is an attractive town with a medieval centre. The town's other claim to fame is its confetti industry, the manufacture of flower-shaped arrangements of sugar-coated almonds, a feature of traditional Italian weddings.

Families will probably be keener to explore the Abruzzi coast which has plenty of good, uncrowded sandy beaches. However there are few genuinely appealing resorts here. The best are probably Alba Adriatica and Pineto. The main town and resort of the Abruzzi coast is Pescara, which is over-crowded and unpleasant in the peak season – but worth a visit if only for its Museo delle Gente d'Abruzzo which is devoted to the life and popular traditions of the region.

MOLISE

This little known part of Italy is far off the tourist trail. It is a wild and sparsely populated region. Its main attraction for tourists are the interesting ruins of a Saepinum, a Roman provincial town – not far from Molise's main town Campobasso. Its main beach resort is Termoli which has a good Romanesque cathedral but there are probably more convenient places to head for if you are just looking for somewhere to bask in the sun.

THE SOUTH

CAMPANIA

This region marks the start of the Italian south – known as the *mezzogiorno*. It used to be an extremely popular destination with the British, once the most popular part of Italy. The names of its resorts are certainly very familiar: Sorrento, Positano, Amalfi and Ravello, for example. And there is Naples, Mt Vesuvius and of course the Roman towns Pompeii and Herculaneum both engulfed by lava in a volcanic eruption in 79AD.

Family holidaymakers are unlikely to head for Naples, as famous for its scruffy, noisy streets and petty crime as it is for its museums and art galleries.

If you are keen to explore the Amalfi cost, Sorrento is the best base. The town has been a resort since Roman times, attracting visitors with its good year-round climate and its attractive cliff-top setting with stunning views over the Bay of Naples.

During the Sixties it attracted the major package holiday companies, but unlike resorts in Spain, Portugal or Greece, Sorrento resisted rapid change – and it still retains some of its old character. It is Italian through and through – lively, colourful, noisy, infuriating and charming in equal parts. Its main drawback, as it is with all the resorts along this coast, is the lack of a decent beach.

Positano, Amalfi and Ravello are also good holiday places. If you want a quiet place, Ravello is probably the best bet.

If you have children who think that Roman civilisation involves the dull study of broken pots and incomplete mosaics, a trip to Pompeii or Herculaneum will provide a stunning glimpse of real everyday Roman life. A trip to the top of Vesuvius – either on foot or by bus – will also make an unforgettable outing.

BASILICATA, APULIA AND CALABRIA

The very southern end of Italy, from the toe of the boot to the heel, is rarely visited by tourists – you will certainly encounter few British visitors in these three regions.

Apulia, the heel, has few towns and cities where you will want to linger: Bari, Taranto and Brindisi are generally unappealing (like many other sea ports and ferry terminals). The white limestone cliffs and plateaux of the Gargano promontory are worth visiting. The coast between Peschici and Vieste has some excellent sandy beaches – Vieste is probably the best place to choose for a beach holiday.

Basilicata is the region that lies between 'toe' and 'heel'. Happily it is no longer the malaria-ridden place inhabited by improvident peasants so vividly described by the writer Carlo Levi in his novel *Christ Stopped at Eboli* (Levi was exiled to Basilicata in the Thirties because of his opposition to Fascism – this provides some idea of exactly how awful this remote region was considered by those in Rome).

It is still poor: there are no grand towns and cities to be visited. It does however have a rich and varied landscape from thick forested hills to deep gorges. There are a couple of stretches of coasts with some small quiet resorts that offer a refreshing contrast to the over-developed seaside places to be found elsewhere in Italy. The Gulf of Policastro on the Tyrrhenian coast and the resort of Maratea are the best places to head for.

Calabria, the toe of Italy, has nearly 400 miles of coastline. The region is over 90 per cent mountain with some peaks reaching to a height of more than 5,000ft. The best of the coastal scenery, and the most appealing of the area's holiday resorts, lie between Pizzo and Scilla. The principal resort is the cliff-top town of Tropea.

8

THE ITALIAN ISLANDS

British travellers are generally familiar with the holiday pleasures of the Greek islands (even if we are not terribly sure
about which is which – in the mind's eye they all tend to blend
into one similar place with a name likely to end in -os). But
what of the Italian islands: we know about Sicily – but is
Sardinia Italian or is it French? Are there any more islands off
the coast of Italy than these?

Most people are surprised to discover that there are quite a
crop of Italian islands (32 to be precise), many of which are
perfect for quiet family holidays (some are penal colonies, so
are less suitable – depending, of course, on your family!).

The islands are all quite different, ranging in size from the
two biggest, Sicily and Sardinia to the smallest which are
barely more than dots in the sea. But whatever the size, unlike
the Greek islands which are often fairly similar in topography
and style, the Italian islands each have their own particular
character and strong identity.

The attraction of a number of them is that their very remote-
ness from the mainland provides them with a special sense of
being away from it all perfect for a relaxing holiday.

SICILY
Unfortunately when most people think of Sicily they tend to
think only of the Mafia whose activities have kept the island in
the news over the past few years. While Sicily has certainly
had its share of troubles, they have rarely affected tourism
(there is street crime on the island – but no more of a problem
than elsewhere in Italy). But the well publicised activities of the
Mafia have combined to affect our perception of the place.
Sicily is in many ways an ideal holiday destination. In
Agrigento and Selinunte, for example, it has some of the finest
archaeological sites in the whole of Europe. And while the

island's beaches are generally unimpressive, it has some charming holiday resorts.

The best of the resorts is Taormina: not beside the sea but a hefty climb up a steep hill. The old town has been attracting discriminating tourists since the turn of the century – Hemingway and D H Lawrence have passed this way. The main attraction is a superb Greek amphitheatre which offers a stunning view of Mt Etna (the amphitheatre is still in regular use for concerts). There are plenty of fine restaurants and lots of good hotels: pricey perhaps but then the best things in life rarely come cheap.

Of the island's other resorts the best is probably Cefalu east of Palermo on the north coast of the island. It has a good wide beach and a pleasant old town centre. At first glance, with its snarling traffic, Palermo might seem rather intimidating. It's worth a longer look. It has plenty of historic sites and lots of attractive old streets and squares. Nearby is the fascinating old town of Monreale with its cathedral built by William II and in which he is buried.

Sicily's principal attraction for children will almost certainly be Mt Etna: nobody of any age can resist a trip up to the steaming top (or as near to the top as you are allowed: see below).

A TRIP UP MOUNT ETNA

There seems to be a fashionable fascination for wanting to climb mountains by the most arduous possible route. Not content with seeking to climb Everest, for example – people want to climb 'Everest: the hard way'.

If ever I were prevailed upon to scale Everest it would have to be 'Everest: the least difficult way possible'. I would demand to be helicoptered to the summit where I would tarry for 10 minutes or so to take a few photos, enjoy a warming draught from a flask of coffee and munch on a couple of Club biscuits.

The helicopter would then whisk me back to the Kathmandu Hilton (or nearest available hostelry of similar standard). Back to my room for a hot bath and a gin and tonic – returned in plenty of time for the early evening news on CNN.

The prospect therefore of a trip up Mount Etna was not one that thrilled. In fact, when it was first suggested, my immediate reaction was to contemplate hiding in a wardrobe until the outing had left without me.

If you were seeking to climb Etna, you would not need to be told that it is a long climb. At 3,350m, Etna is the largest volcano in Europe and one of the largest in the world. Lounging in an easy chair on a sun-bathed hotel terrace beside the sea in Taormina, one can gaze on Etna in all its majesty. It has a pleasing sugar loaf mass; and its volcanic cone sending up a billowing head of steam is a delight to watch. But as I sat there with a glass of Corvo wine, a bowl of olives and *Barchester Towers* on my lap, I thought of the words of Sir Edmund Hillary who was asked why he had climbed Everest. 'Because it was there,' he said. A perfectly good reason to have left the thing alone I would have said.

The schedule for the Etna expedition was reasonably demanding: leave after breakfast, up and down the mountain before lunch, lunch on the descent, back to the hotel late afternoon. Bring a warm coat and wear a pair of stout shoes. No need, apparently, for karabiners, crampons, pitons, sherpas, ice-picks or anything else which smacks of Chris Bonnington with an iced-up beard and 'Everest: the hard way'. I felt sufficiently encouraged to sign up.

Wednesday

8.00am
A light breakfast. My thoughts keep returning to the mountain and the rigours of the ascent ahead. I check and re-check my equipment: an apple, five Baci chocolates, *Barchester Towers*, a tube of sun block and a Sony Walkman.

8.30am
Board the bus; nervous laughter as we take our seats. On the drive I eat the apple and two of the chocolates. Finish *Barchester Towers* and the batteries in the Walkman run out. First blood to the Mountain.

As the bus chugs up the lower slopes, time to reflect on Etna's rich history. The Ancient Greeks believed Etna to be the forge of Vulcan and the home of the Cyclops. Pindar called it 'the Pillar of Heaven'. The Greek philosopher Empedocles made a close study of the volcano, living in an observatory near the summit. He must have been overworking because he eventually formed the belief that if he jumped into the crater the escaping mass of gas would support his weight. Old Emp jumped in but all that later came out was one of his bronze sandals.

Driving up the volcano, lava from previous eruptions can be seen everywhere. The black rock has been imaginitively recycled to build garden walls and even entire houses. History suggests that the volcano is more dangerous to tourists (nine visitors were killed in 1979, two in 1987) than it is to local residents. The flow of lava moves too slowly to take anybody much by surprise. The most recent eruption earlier this year was spectacular but seems to have caused little damage.

10.30am

We reach base camp: Rifugio Sapienza, about a mile below the summit. Here some of the hardest climbing awaits us: a couple of dozen fairly steep steps up to the cable car station. I feel slightly breathless; probably from a lack of oxygen.

The cable car, now back in business after being destroyed in the last major eruption of 1983, speeds us dramatically up the mountain.

10.45am

Almost journey's end! The cable car sets us down at a refuge where you can buy a drink and rent warm clothing. We pause for a *cappuccino* before boarding a bus which chugs asthmatically up a steep incline through a barren lunar landscape towards the summit.

11am

Where the bus drops us off is a large sign: 'The guardians will not answer for the safety of tourists not equipped with windcheaters and heavy boots.' Walking by the sign were crowds of people in open-necked shirts and equipped in nothing stouter than sand-shoes.

Now for the assault on the summit. I finish off the Baci chocolates, zip up my coat and follow the path. Walking over the lava is like running up the school coke heap. We pass another sign in several languages which reads: 'May peace prevail on earth.' Yeah, like, really nice.

The drop in temperature is extraordinary. Even though the sun beams brightly from a cloudless sky, the wind cuts like a knife up here. The people in the open-necked shirts hunch their shoulders against the chill.

So near to the summit, but yet so far. After a five-minute walk and in sight of the crater, a rope bars the way with a notice warning that it would be highly dangerous to proceed further. Denied our final triumph, our expedition which had departed with such high hopes trudges back down towards the bus station. On the bus we nurse our disappointment with surprising fortitude. A man from Leeds considers the whole venture a complete waste of time. 'What were there to see up there? Nowt! Bloody nothing. Lot of bloody black rock and some bloody steam coming out of the ground. I don't call that much! I don't rate that at all.'

Two women from Lucerne smugly admit to having walked up. 'We make the hike,' she said, adding unnecessarily: 'This is a walk for serious hikers only.'

1pm
Our expedition has safely returned back down the cable car to Rifugio Sapienza. We linger to buy ashtrays made out of lava and postcards showing horrific scenes of the erupting crater. We are glad we heeded the advice not to cross the rope.

To celebrate our safe deliverance from the Forge of Vulcan we repair to a restaurant where with hearty appetites we devour plates of pasta, several bottles of house red and generous portions of sweetmeats from the trolley.

3pm
I doze pleasurably as the bus returns to the hotel at Taormina. I plan my moving account: *Etna: the easy way*.

SARDINIA
In many ways Sardinia is the least Italian of all the Italian islands, a fact explained by its distance from the Italian mainland – halfway between Italy and North Africa. Compared with other Mediterranean islands such as French-owned Corsica, Sardinia has been less developed by the holiday companies.

It is a big island, about 150 miles long and 75 miles wide, with a coastline of around 800 miles. However tourist development has mainly been concentrated on a few small areas.

Alghero in the north-east, with an attractive town centre, is the island's biggest resort. The best beach, a three mile stretch of white sand, starts from about a mile north of Alghero.

On the north-east coast, the choice of the resorts is probably Baia Sardinia which has an attractive white sand beach and a bustling city centre with plenty of activity in the evening. Nearby is the best known tourist development on the island which lies along the Costa Smeralda. At its heart is Porto Cervo with a big marina and a clutch of up-market hotels.

In the south of the island the majority of the tourist development lies around Cagliari, the island's capital, worth visiting for its excellent National Archaeological Museum with its famous collection of bronze figures.

West of Cagliari near Santa Margherita is the highly-rated Forte Hotel Village which offers guests a wide range of sporting activities at an all-inclusive price. Also worth considering is the small town of Sant'Antioco with its tree-lined main street.

ELBA

Elba lies eight miles off the coast of Tuscany: at 18 miles long and 12 miles wide, it is Italy's third largest island after Sicily and Sardinia. The island is reach by ferry from Livorno (journey time: three hours); from Piombino (one hour); and Porto Santo Stefano (one hour).

If we know it at all in Britain it is because it was here that Napoleon was once exiled (celebrated in the famous Napoleon palindrome: 'Able was I ere I saw Elba').

Compared with the overcrowded, unimpressive resorts on the Tuscan mainland, Elba offers unspoilt beaches and complete peace and quiet. There is little nightlife and no real sights. The best of the resorts is probably Procchil and the best of the island's beaches are to be found at Fetovaia and Biodola.

CAPRI

The isle of Capri has always had a particular fascination for the British. This is where the singer Gracie Fields and the composer Sir William Walton ended their days; George Bernard Shaw, D H Lawrence and Graham Greene have also been visitors. Even Lenin came here.

Its proximity to Naples and Sorrento, from which it is served by ferries and hydrofoils (every hour in the summer: hydrofoils take 40 mins, steamers 1hr 15mins), means that the island has a regular supply of trippers. If you don't like crowds you would be advised to give the place a miss during July and August or on summer weekends in other months.

What brings so many people to Capri is plain to see: despite the development (or over-development depending on your point of view), Capri has retained its good looks – and its sea views remain as stunning as ever.

ISCHIA

A near neighbour to Capri in the Bay of Naples, Ischia may be lesser known and less glamorous but in many ways it offers more attractions, particularly for a family holiday. Unlike Capri, for example, it has good long beaches.

Regular ferries and hydrofoils from Naples and other points on the mainland bring travellers to the island (hydrofoils take from 40 minutes, steamers take from 80 minutes).

Ischia has always had a faithful following, particularly among Germans, for its thermal springs and treatments involving mud baths.

Most of the tourist development on the island is concentrated on the northern and western sides, the most attractive part of Ischia is to be found on the southern side. Its most attractive resort is Sant'Angelo with some jolly cafes and a crop of agreeable hotels.

GIGLIO

Giglio, next to Elba, is the largest of the Tuscan islands. It is about twelve-and-a-half miles long and five miles wide. The word 'giglio' means lily: while much of the island is green and attractive, there are substantial barren stretches and few worthwhile beaches. In the summer there are daily ferries to Giglio from Porto S Stefano on the mainland.

PONZA

This is the main island of the Pontine group – a sprinkling of islands scattered across the sea between Rome and Naples.

111

Only two are inhabited, and Ponza is the only one worth visiting. It is five miles long and one mile wide. The main town is Ponza with a surprisingly wide array of shops and a good clean beach. The island is reached by steamer (journey time: one hour) and hydrofoil (70 minutes) from Formia and Anzio on the mainland.

AEOLIAN ISLANDS

These islands which lie off the coast of northern Sicily take their name from the Greek god Aeolus who kept the winds under his control, locked in a cave on one of the islands. Greek myth or not, the islands certainly do get their share of stiff breezes.

As holiday places they are known only to the Italians, who tend to visit only in July and August. But even in high season you are unlikely to find yourself in teeming crowds. There are seven main islands in the group: Lipari, Vulcano, Salina, Panarea, Filicudi, Alicudi and Stromboli. There are year-round ferry and hydrofoil services from Milazzo and summer services from Naples, Reggio di Calabria and Messina: the nearest island to the Sicilian mainland is Vulcano, about 90 minutes away by ferry.

The largest of the islands, and the most popular with tourists, is Lipari which has an attractive main town with some good hotels. Canneto is a fishing village with a pebbled beach and a couple of good hotels.

Stromboli is probably the best known island in the Aeolian group for its active volcano. As a volcanic island, like all the islands, its beaches are black but perfectly satisfactory. The highlight of any stay is a trip up to the observatory to watch the volcano's own firework show, best seen at night.

EGADI ISLANDS

Situated off the west coast of Sicily, the three Egadi islands are easily reached. The main island Favignana is just 25 minutes by hydrofoil from Trapani. Most visitors are day-trippers who come to enjoy the sun on the island's handful of rocky beaches. The island of Levanzo is more reminiscent of a Greek island with its white houses. The third island Marettimo, is the furthest away, and is the least developed.

9

CITY BREAKS

Almost any Italian town or city you care to choose would make a perfect base for a weekend break: you can be sure of finding a good, well-run hotel; fine, good value restaurants; and a stack of fascinating things to look at ranging from Etruscan pots to Renaissance paintings.

But we have chosen three cities which we recommend as the top choice for a short break. Rome and Venice pick themselves – along with Paris, they are arguably *the* top three European destinations. Milan may not seem an obvious choice, but it has a number of compelling attractions. It's a short flight from the UK (90 minutes from London), it's a marvellous city with a multitude of attractions (ranging from opera at La Scala to football at San Siro) and is well placed for a quick trip out to the Lakes.

ROME

We often like to kid ourselves that foreign travel with children is an improving experience for them. Even a trip to Lloret de Mar we are sure will provide the little ones with some sort of invaluable educational input. Unfortunately, from most foreign trips the only lasting thing of any significance that many children get is a sun tan and the occasional dose of holiday tummy.

A short trip to Rome is quite a different kettle of holiday fish. For almost any subject on the national curriculum, a stay in Rome will almost certainly offer your child valuable educational input. Certainly there is plenty of ancient history to be devoured (you can't turn a corner in the city without bumping into some important piece of Roman remains).

And whatever else you learn in Rome, you can brush up on a few clichés – the city is cliché capital of the world. I ran through a few for my children. Rome wasn't built in a day. When in Rome, do as the Romans do. All roads lead to Rome. The children disputed this last observation. The road at the end of our drive doesn't lead to Rome, they pointed out, it leads to the centre of Bath. Well, the road from Leonardo da Vinci airport leads to Rome. Or at least that was our hope. The taxi driver at the airport made it obvious that having to stop to pick us up was spoiling his day. I loaded the bags into the boot and climbed into the front passenger seat beside him.

'Holiday Inn,' I said.

'Hummff,' said the taxi driver and looked away. He jabbed a finger to set the meter rolling. It began to run up a bill in lire, several digits at a time. This wasn't a taxi fare: as the total mounted it looked as if I was being asked to settle the entire national debt of Bolivia.

He then turned up the radio so loud that the plastic ornaments on the dashboard threatened to explode. I had a moment of doubt – as I do in all my dealings with foreign taxi drivers: had he really understood where I wanted to go?

'Holiday Inn?' I said again, inserting a hanging interrogative.

'Hummff!!!' he snorted. I had the impression that I was beginning to get on his nerves. The radio was turned up another dozen decibels. In terms of volume it was like sitting in the front row of an Iron Maiden concert.

Clear of the airport precincts, the battered yellow Fiat suddenly bolted forward as if an afterburner had been ignited – like that moment on Concorde when you feel a slight nudge in the seat of your pants as the plane pushes through the sound barrier, we were pinned back with G-Force as the taxi nipped into the fast lane of the motorway.

The drive into town was that old, speeded up film of a train ride from London to Brighton in one-and-a-half minutes. If I'd felt that anyone could have heard me over the noise of the radio I might have screamed. This was the road to Hell.

We arrived. The taxi driver looked at the fare on the meter and through some arcane process of computation known only to the international fraternity of taxi drivers, told me that I had to pay nearly twice as much as the amount shown. Despite being limp from the terror of the ride from the airport, I dared to query his arithmetic: 'This seems to be rather more than the fare shown on the meter. . .'

'Hummff!!!' explained the taxi driver. This was not the noblest Roman of them all. He snatched the bundle of notes I offered and sped from the hotel with a Batmobile handbrake turn, burning rubber.

The idea of the Holiday Inn St Peter's conjured up images from a Fellini film. A reception desk manned by cardinals; nuns working as chamber maids; holy water on tap; a Sistine Chapel suite; gregorian chants in the lift. Hang a sign on your bedroom door: 'Ready to be confessed'. But it was just another Holiday Inn with a lobby full of Chinese flight attendants fighting over their luggage.

Next morning the lobby was full of Indian flight attendants arguing about their mini-bar bills. We rode the hotel shuttle bus as far as St Peter's (it's a curious rule of hotels that their names generally have little to do with their geographical location: the Holiday Inn St Peter's is of course at least a 10 minute bus drive from St Peter's).

In Rome the city centre traffic runs at the same speed as on the motorway: 0–75mph in six seconds. Pedestrians and cyclists live on borrowed time. There are old pedestrians and bold pedestrians: but not many old, bold pedestrians. And the life expectancy of someone driving a Vespa scooter down the Via del Corso can probably be measured like that of a First World War pilot: in hours and minutes.

Car parking techniques are certainly not included in the Italian driving test. Double parking is normal. But most extraordinary are the drivers who fill the last tiny gap on a street by frantically driving their car in at a 90 degree angle, beaching their car up on the pavement like a D-Day landing craft, the bonnet hard against the wall. God knows how blind people or those in wheelchairs manage to get around here.

St Peter's and the Sistine Chapel

The Romans would probably try to get their cars into St Peter's Basilica if it weren't for the steps. The traffic jam at the entrance to the church was caused by a crush of Japanese crowded around Michelangelo's magnificent Pieta. The Pieta is hard to see nowadays as it sits behind a glass screen following a sledgehammer attack on it a few years ago. When the Japanese start popping their flashlights you can see nothing beyond the reflected bright white holes that the flashlights burn into your retina.

Very big, St Peter's. You might profitably decide to take the quickest of looks and move on. If you feel energetic you can climb to the top of the dome for stunning views of the city. However you will probably need to conserve your energy for the long walk to the Vatican museum and the even longer walk through the museum into the Sistine chapel and back out again.

If you've got 12 years to spare you would have the time to see all the riches of the Vatican Museum. Amongst the huge Papal treasure trove there are Raphaels, Donatellos, Michelangelos and Leonardos – but to the chagrin of our children, not a Teenage Mutant Ninja Turtle in sight. (Hey dudes, this is no Leonardo cartoon!)

The Sistine Chapel is named after Pope Sixtus IV whose nephew Pope Julius commissioned Michelangelo to decorate the ceiling. Julius envisaged something relatively modest: what he got was sensational. He started out with the idea of painting the Twelve Apostles but then embarked on an extraordinary depiction of the Old Testament from the Creation to the Flood. Michelangelo worked on it for four years driving Pope Julius II mad with impatience to see the completed work: 'When will you finish,' he demanded. 'When I can,' the artist kept replying. (Rome wasn't built in a day. The clichés have their point!) The recent controversial restoration, financed by a Japanese TV company, reveals the work in its original loud colours (lots of bright yellows, greens and purple). The only problem is the pain in the neck you get from staring up at the ceiling for so long.

'I'm museum-ed out,' said the American woman next to me in the chapel. 'I just had to take three hours: hey, you know, time out! I had to say: "That's enough renaissance art for me today!" Oh boy!'

'You're telling me,' said her friend. 'I don't mind walking. I like walking. But boy my feet. You wanna Lifesaver?'

That evening, sitting on the shuttle bus in the city centre waiting to go back to the hotel, we watched an affluent young couple dressed up for a night out. A gypsy boy appeared from out of the darkness, inviting them to buy something he held in his hands. Displaying an extraordinary swiftness of movement, the girl leapt behind her male companion – pushing her handbag out of sight and deftly removing her earrings.

'Cultural stereotypes are evil, as we all know,' write Dana Facaros and Michael Pauls in *Cadogan Walks: Rome* (Cadogan, £8.95), 'but when you see gypsies in Rome, jam a hand in your crucial pocket and be ready to kick or bash anyone that comes close.' When in Rome, do as the Romans do (watch them clichés come down). If you're travelling around Rome – or anywhere else in the world nowadays – take only those replaceable things that you can afford to have stolen. Leave your valuables in the hotel safe.

The Colosseum and Ancient Rome

The next day when we were walking near the Colosseum, we were well prepared when a gang of gypsy children swarmed around. I acted with calm measured authority: I screamed and ran. It proved an effective deterrent – the gypsy children were astonished by such craven behaviour.

If the Vatican is hard work, Ancient Rome is even more of a foot-slog. When I was a much younger man, I could have translated into Latin: "Know thee that Rome is built on seven hills." Now I could just about manage to climb a few of them: the Palatine, the Capitoline, the Esquiline, the Aventine *et al* (to use the Latin). There is no packaging of Rome's ancient treasures: no interpretative centres, nobody dressed in a toga, no 'living history'. The old Colosseum and Forum are part of the city centre, they seem to have a respectable life of their own. They are open to tourists but tourists are offered no special favours: you can take them or leave them.

Rome is a perfect city for a short break because, away from the madcap traffic, it is ideal for aimless wandering. Fine old streets and squares run into each other, each one more intriguing than the last. Interesting shops: this one selling outfits for the well-dressed parish priest, the place next door stocked with exquisitely well designed light fittings. Good bars and restaurants.

The other main sights

There are surprisingly few 'must see' sights. The Piazza Navona is a very attractive Baroque piazza that echoes the shape of Domitian's stadium that once stood on this spot and where athletic contests were held before crowds of over 30,000.

The Trevi fountain, famous for the films *Three Coins in the Fountain* and Fellini's classic of Rome life in the Sixties *La Dolce Vita* is a grand architectural confection. But most people come in order to toss a coin into its waters, which will apparently guarantee their return. It's a lively spot to come to in the evenings (though you are unlikely to see Anita Ekberg splashing around in it as she did in *La Dolce Vita*).

Another popular gathering place – day or night – are the Spanish Steps. Have a look at the excellent museum in Keats' House at 26 Piazza di Spagna.

For a spot of the bizarre, take a trip out to the Olympic stadium where Lazio and Roma football clubs play: the pedestrian approach is decorated with an extraordinary mosaic praising the dubious achievements of *Il Duce*: the main theme is Mussolini's inglorious conquest of Abyssinia.

The supreme attraction of Rome is that unlike Paris or Florence you don't feel you're shirking your tourist duty if you simply walk the streets. The area around the Campo dei Fiori has a particularly good laid-back atmosphere where you feel you could spend all day in cafes drinking *cappuccino* and eating slices of pizza – looking cool in your Ray-Bans.

Out of town
The one outing we undertook was a drive down the old Appian Way. I hired a car for the day and braved the mad traffic. The Via Appia: 'the Queen of Roads', was built in 312 BC by Consul Appius Claudius, and originally linked Rome to Capua. Later it was extended onwards to the port of Brindisi to serve Rome's newly conquered empire in the east. The Via Appia was a sort of Roman motorway: 4 metres wide with two pavements on either side and as straight as an arrow. The old road starts at the Caracalla baths, scene of the famous Pavarotti, Carreras and Domingo World Cup concert. Only a mile or so from the Colosseum, yet you feel you are deep in the Italian countryside.

Shortly after the Porta di San Sebastiano is the spot where St Peter, who was fleeing from persecution in Rome, is said to have met Christ on the road and asked him: *'Domine, quo vadis?'* (Lord, where are you going?) Christ replied that he was going to Rome in order to be crucified for a second time. Christ disappeared, St Peter turned back to Rome and was crucified himself. And producers of Biblical film epics were eternally grateful.

A few hundred yards further on are the Catacombs, a series of underground Christian cemeteries which date back to the Third Century. The biggest of these subterranean cemeteries is St Callistus' Catacombs.

Our guide was a young Italian who spoke American English with a Robert de Niro delivery. We descended underground into a labyrinth of dimly lit galleries, each with hundreds of tombs hewn out of the rock. In the St Callistus catacomb altogether there are some half a million tombs.

'Robert de Niro' pointed out the symbolic paintings with his torch: 'This is Jonah. He's in the whale, right? That means the promise of resurrection . . . A man with a lamb. Christ saving the lost soul, right?' There are tombs, tombs and tombs. 'I know what you're thinking. Where are all the bones, right?' The bones have been moved out to stop the school kids nicking them. And at the end: 'Hey, enjoy the rest of your holiday, right?'

A short way down the road is the Circus Maxentius, the extensive remains of a hippodrome built for chariot racing. Not quite on the Ben Hur scale of Circus Maximus in the centre of Rome, which accommodated up to 250,000 people, the Circus Maxentius is breathtakingly well preserved and seems to see few tourists. (There is not even a car park.)

The Via Appia continues south. With the original Roman paving stones still in place on a number of stretches of road, it is hardly much different from the way it must have looked 2000 years ago. Well, one or two differences. Romans drive out along the road to park and wash their cars. And to indulge in other less salubrious pursuits. The first come-on that I received I assumed was a genial greeting. The second invitation was much more sexually explicit and admitted no confusion. It was incredible: these were women of retirement age and hideous to an astonishing degree. Men were parking their cars and accompanying the ladies behind the ancient tombs which line the Appian Way. Further along there were younger, more attractive women who, on second looks, were transvestites. But on this ancient highway, perhaps it was ever thus.

Just at the moment when the Appian Way starts to get really fascinating, Rome's equivalent of the M25 suddenly barges across it leaving no way to cross the dual carriageway without making a five-mile detour. Britain's Department of Transport is road mad but probably not mad enough to run a motorway right over one of the most famous roads in the world.

When we returned for the flight home, Fiumcino airport was thick with men and women in uniform toting sub-machine guns, a load of Common Market big-wigs were expected. All roads still lead to Rome, I sagely announced.

It was time for a Rome cliché test. 'Rome wasn't built in a...?' In a hurry?' offered the children. Well, close enough: when did builders ever hurry? That's a cliché any child ought to learn.

VENICE

Like Rome, one of the attractions of a short break in Venice is that you are under no compulsion to race around the city attempting to take in all the sights, it is enough simply to wander around the city going where your fancy takes you. And in Venice the fancy will take you quite a long way.

Of course, you will probably want to see St Mark's Square, the Doges' Palace and the Accademia (and they are all well worth seeing) but nothing will give you quite so much pleasure as simply enjoying the city as a whole. The two things that you will certainly need to get the most out of Venice are a good city map and a stout pair of walking shoes. Over two days you will walk as much as you have ever walked in your life, and even with a good map I can guarantee that you will get lost fairly frequently. But getting lost in Venice is half the fun of the place. It is hard to get completely lost. There are three Venetian landmarks which are signposted everywhere: the Ferrovia (the railway station); St Mark's Square; and the Rialto Bridge – the trick is to get your bearings in relation to these main points.

The best way to arrive in Venice is by boat (if you fly to Venice's Marco Polo airport, the water bus from the airport brings you via the Lido straight to St Mark's Square). That first sight of the city from across the sea is unforgettable. A couple of hours before you were in the very real world of Britain and now you are drawing closer to a city that looks wholly unreal. It takes a second or two to realise that part of what makes the place look so unreal is that there are no cars to be seen. (It's surprising how quickly you adjust to life without cars.)

As far as the eye can see, there are wonderful palaces and magnificent churches with their rounded domes, all looking serene and marvellous beside the canals. It is almost as if you have arrived in an adult version of Euro Disney. Surely it is all too good to be true.

But as you get off the boat and find your way to your hotel, and as you pick your way along empty echoing passageways and across silent bridges, you begin to discover that the place is even more wonderful than it looked from the boat.

If you are driving to Venice you will come to the city from the mainland via the causeway and you will probably park in the big multi-storey park at Piazzale Roma. Coming by car destroys the illusion of Venice to some extent: entering by boat you can kid yourself that Venice is not properly part of the real world. But this shattered illusion does not last long: within a couple of hours, the magic of Venice has gathered you up and swept you along. For as long as you are in Venice, you remain firmly rooted in another world.

The fact that the main Santa Lucia station is within easy distance of St Mark's Square (not more than 30 minutes on foot, about 10 minutes by vaporetto water bus), makes the train an excellent way of getting to the city. If you are on holiday in somewhere like Milan or Verona, you could fit in a long day-trip to Venice as an outing.

The main sights
Start at St Mark's Square (described as "the largest drawing room in Europe") which is as about as central as you can get in a city as spread-out as Venice is. Altogether there are around 120 islands which make up Venice, and in total there are some 150 canals which are crossed by more than 400 bridges. (The sprawl of the city however is deceptive: from St Mark's Square nowhere is more than 30 minutes' walk away (the relative compactness of the place explains why you can do and see so much in such a short stay). St Mark's Square is where the trip-pers gather, so if you want to see it at its best come early or come very late (some argue that it is a place best enjoyed when it's empty and bathed in moonlight).

The Basilica is impressive from the outside – inside it is dark and rather gloomy: however the ceiling has some fabulous gold mosaics of angels and saints, and the floors are carpeted with extraordinary mosaics. The Doges' Palace was the seat of the Venetian government and magistrature: amongst other things it housed the armouries, courtrooms and dungeons.

The Doges' Palace is connected to the neighbouring jail by the famous Bridge of Sighs: so-called 'for the sigh heaved by a prisoner fresh from the courtroom of the palace, who crosses the canal by this bridge on his way to serve a long sentence in a foul, dank dungeon: through the lattice window the wretch catches sights of the Lagoon, of the Island of San Giorgio, of the sky and the sunshine outside'. The state rooms are open to the public and are worth seeing for their wonderfully orna-mented ceilings.

Almost every side street (if street is the right word for Venice) has a church or palace. Certainly there will be a clutch of shops, a cheerful cafe, a good restaurant almost at every turn. This is why what you intend to be a short stroll quickly develops into mini-marathon. But never will a walk have been quite so much fun.

Almost any district of Venice has something of interest. One of my favourite parts is the old Ghetto in Cannaregio (this was the original Ghetto which gave the infamous name to the world). The area still retains a distinctive character, serene and mysterious, quite different from anywhere else in the city.

Of the city's museums the star attraction is undoubtedly the Accademia which has a rich collection of Venetian art including works by Bellini, Giorgione and Veronese. The museum that children will most enjoy is the Naval Museum near the Arsenal.

Children will also appreciate a ride out in a ferry boat across the bay to one of the islands. On Murano you can see the glass factory; Burano is visited for its lace schools; while Torcello has no particular attraction, it is simply exceptionally pretty. If you want to lie on a beach, take the vaporetto (line 1 or 2) and head for the Lido.

The canals

The best of all sights in Venice is the Grand Canal, and can be enjoyed from various vantage points (the Rialto bridge, for example) free of charge – or, for the price of a ticket, from the deck of a water bus. While the Grand Canal is Venice's star canal, there are plenty of others which you will enjoy even more.

The extraordinary thing about the city is that while the main tourist places like St Mark's Square and the Rialto bridge get clogged up with visitors, it is quite easy to leave them behind by exploring the small alleys that lead off the busy thoroughfares.

Of course to get around the city, there are no four-wheel buses and no taxis (certainly no underground!): the only trans-port are the water buses and water taxis. Even if you are not planning to go anywhere in particular, the water buses (*vaporetti*) do not exactly offer a rapid transit system, but they are great fun to use and certainly offer the best way of seeing the city from the water.

Unless you have money to burn, don't be tempted to take a trip in a gondola which probably rank as one of the greatest rip-offs in international tourism. Expect to pay from around £50. To get a gondola experience at a bargain price, take a trip on a *traghetto* – the gondola ferries which are used to cross the Grand Canal (they are signposted with distinctive yellow signs. These cost around 50p per crossing.)

The two main vaporetti lines of use to tourists are Line 1 called the 'Accelerato', which contrary to its name, is actually quite slow stopping at all the stops along the Grand Canal between the Piazzale Roma and the Lido. Line 2 is faster and more expensive and stops only at Ferrovia (the railway station), Piazzale Roma, Zattere, San Marco, San Zaccaria and the Lido. It is probably best to invest in a ticket valid for 24 hours which costs around £5 (a three-day ticket costs around £8). Tickets can be bought from almost any landing stage.

If you want transport faster than a vaporetto, you will have to dig deeper in your pocket for a *motoscafo* (water taxi). Even shortish trips start at around £20.

MILAN
In many ways Milan is a perfect contrast to Rome and Venice. While these two cities symbolise the wealth of Italy's history, Milan is the present and future of the country. It is the financial capital of Italy – the stock exchange is based here – and it is the engine of the once much-vaunted Italian economic miracle.

Certainly, there are plenty of grand old buildings here, but here they compete for attention with less appealing modern structures. But it is not so much the physical appearance of the city that the short-break visitor should come to enjoy, Milan's greatest asset is its exuberant style.

Another bonus is that the majority of the city's main sights are all grouped together in centre within a short walk of each other. If you don't want to walk Milan boasts one of Europe's most efficient public transport systems, featuring trams, buses and an underground metro.

The main sights
Start in the Piazza del Duomo, the heart of the city, where you can enjoy the impressive façade of the Duomo, the largest gothic cathedral in the world. Among the Duomo's religious

treasures is a crucifix, hung high above the chancel, which is claimed to have a nail from Christ's cross (which Emperor Constantine is said to have turned into a bit for his horse). The cross is lowered each year using a device invented by Leonarda da Vinci.

Across the piazza is the magnificent Galleria Vittorio Emmanuele, a cross-shaped glass-topped gallery containing shops and restaurants (prices are as you might expect in such a top spot). Walk through the Galleria to reach the Piazza della Scala where you will find the famous opera house (where tickets are expensive and hard to get). The opera season runs from December to July – and there is normally a programme of classical music concerts from September to November. The box office is situated at La Scala, Via de Filodrammatici 2, Milan (Tel: 7200 3744; fax 887 9297) and is open daily from 10am to 1pm and from 3pm to 6pm. You can often manage to get a seat in the gods sold on the day – 200 standing places are also made available. You should get there about an hour before the performance begins.

If you don't manage to enjoy an opera, you can at least visit the museum which provides a chance to spy the auditorium (which has tiers of boxes but no circle). Among the museum's exhibits are casts of conductor Toscanini's hands, a piano used by Lizst and a statue of Puccini in a voluminous overcoat.

Without doubt Milan's star tourist attraction is Leonardo's *Last Supper*, not a conventional painting on canvas as many people think but a mural to be found on a wall in the refectory of the convent next door to the church of Santa Maria delle Grazie. The *Last Supper* (signposted *Cenacolo Vinciano* in Italian) may be Milan's best-known work of art – but there is much else to be enjoyed by the art lover.

The best of the art galleries is the Pinacoteca di Brera which has an enormous selection of paintings, ranging from modern work by Modigliani, De Chirico and Carra to Renaissance Venetian artists like Bonifacio and Giovanni's famous *Pieta*. Other art galleries worth seeking out include the Civica Galleria d'Arte Moderne (with paintings by Corot, Millet and the French Impressionists).

One of the best treats for weekend breakers is Milan's shopping. The Quadrilatero area is the place to head for, located around Via Monte Napoleone. Here you will find the big-name Italian fashion designers. Designer cast-offs can be bought at the early morning Saturday market on Viale Papiniano close to the Porta Genova railway station.

Out of Town
Train journeys from Milan are cheap, making it possible to attempt easy day trips to nearby places. For example, Stresa on Lake Maggiore is just an hour away by express train, with a return fare of around £12. Pavia is a beautiful medieval city just 20 miles from Milan and well worth a visit. Why not go to the Stazione Centrale and play a sort of day-trip Russian roulette and simply jump on the first train to the most likely looking place no more than an hour's ride away. Wherever you end up, such is the charm of Italy, you are sure not to be disappointed.

10

DIRECTORY OF ITALIAN SPECIALIST OPERATORS

For each operator we show whether it is a member of ABTA (Association of British Travel Agents), has an Air Tour Organiser's Licence (ATOL), or whether it belongs to the Association of Independent Tour Operators (AITO): all of which guarantee that a company is bonded. Under European legislation all companies offering package travel should offer such protection but the law is patchily enforced – it would be wise to check with any operator before booking. For all purchases over £100 made with a credit card (Access or Visa), you are protected under the Consumer Credit Act. If the operator goes bust you can recover your money from the credit card company.

As well as a brief description of each company, the listing shows under which other sections of this book you can find more information about the holidays it offers.

1st Roman Breaks
Smitham House,
127 Brighton Road, Coulsdon,
Surrey CR5 2NJ
Admin: 081-660 0082
Res: 081-660 0082
Fax: 081-660 2306
'Established in 1988, 1st Roman Breaks is an independent tour operator specialising in the letting of holiday flats/houses to individuals, families or larger groups. Accommodation is principally in and around Rome, although in 1994 we are also going to offer accommodation in Florence and Tuscany. In 1993, around 800 persons have visited Rome with 1st Roman Breaks. The firm specialises in holidays or short lets although longer periods can be arranged for students or academics. Accommodation only is provided in the package but assistance can be given with flights if necessary. All properties have been personally inspected.'
Self-catering holidays: Rome & surrounding region, Florence

A T Mays City Breaks
21 Royal Crescent,
Glasgow G3 7SZ
Admin: 041 331 1200
Res: 041 331 1121
Fax: 041 332 0563
ABTA: 49712
ATOL: 0020
Credit cards: VISA ACCESS
AMEX DINERS
'City Breaks is a division of A
T Mays, the fourth largest
multiple travel agent in the
UK. It has been established
for six years. We carry over
10,000 passengers every year
to 23 destinations including
Rome, Florence and Venice.
Our clients can choose to
concentrate on seeing one city
or combine two or three destinations in a multi-centre
holiday. Our packages include
scheduled flight departures
from 25 UK airports and hotel
accommodation in a range of
categories, from two star to
five star deluxe. Our hotels
are all centrally located and
we can also arrange reasonably priced excursions. For
groups of 10 or more people
travelling together, our
Groups Department organises
departures to all our city
break destinations.'
Special interest holidays: City
breaks

AA Driveaway
AA Motoring Holidays,
Automobile Association
Developments, PO Box 128
Fanum House, Basingstoke
RG21 2AE
Admin: 0256 493878
Res: 0256 493878
ABTA: 65626
Credit cards: VISA ACCESS
The AA in its Driveaway
programme offers short breaks
and hotel touring holidays.
'As well as the ferry crossing,
we book all your chosen
hotels in advance. You can
book as many hotels as you
like and stay in each hotel as
long as you wish. You can
also add on extra nights with
any of the other hotel groups
or countries in our brochure.
Another option is our go-as-
you-please programme. Here
we only book your ferry
crossing and you take nightly
vouchers accepted by all
hotels in Italy belonging to the
same hotel group.'
Hotel holidays: All over Italy

Abercrombie & Kent
Sloane Square House, Holbein
Place, London SW1W 8NS
Admin: 071-730 9600
Res: 071-730 9600
Fax: 071-730 9376
ABTA: 72314
Credit cards: VISA ACCESS
'Abercrombie & Kent's selec-
tion of their favourite hotels,
castles and villas are spread

throughout key and growing areas of interest. We offer elegant architecture, rooms with views of idyllic landscapes, gourmet or local food and a warm welcome from owners and staff.' Destinations include the Italian Lakes, the Dolomite mountain ranges, the Veneto, Umbria and Sicily.

Hotel holidays: All over Italy

Aeroscope

Scope House, Hospital Road, Moreton-in-Marsh, Glos GL56 0BQ
Admin: 0608 50103
Res: 0608 50103
Fax: 0608 51295
ABTA: 74061
ATOL: 1377
Credit cards: VISA ACCESS
'Aeroscope has been established for nearly 14 years and is fully bonded and licensed with ABTA, IATA and the CAA. It caters for holiday-makers and travellers who primarily are independently-minded and like to do their own thing. Aeroscope is a provider of competitive air fares throughout Europe and provides accommodation, if required, in any one of 800 Best Western hotels as well as a wide choice of youth and family hostels for the budget conscious.'

Special interest holidays: City breaks

Airtours

Wavell House, Holcombe Road, Helmshore, Rossendale BB4 4NB
Admin: 0706 830130
Res: 0706 260000
ATOL: 1379
Credit cards: VISA ACCESS
Britain's second largest tour operator features Italy in a programme of lakes and mountains holidays as well as offering sun and sand packages.

Hotel holidays: Lakes, Naples and surrounding region, Adriatic Coast
Special interest holidays: Coach holidays

Allegro Holidays

Vanguard House, 277 London Road, Burgess Hill, West Sussex RH15 9QU
Admin: 0444 235678
Res: 0444 248222
Fax: 0444 235789
ABTA: 12173
ATOL: 1835
AITO
Credit cards: VISA ACCESS AMEX
'Allegro Holidays is a specialist in the north-western part of Sardinia. The company offers a wide selection of mainly family-run hotels and apartments (all with pools) in or near the medieval town of Alghero, on the Coral Coast. Allegro's Mediterranean Gems brochure is the only one to list

direct flights from Gatwick, Manchester and Glasgow.'
Hotel holidays: Sardinia
Self-catering holidays: Sardinia

Andante Travels
Grange Cottage,
Winterbourne Dauntsey,
Salisbury SP4 6ER
Admin: 0980 610555
Res: 0980 610555
'Andante Travels is a small, specialist company offering holidays and tours in art and archaeology. We take small parties with a guide lecturer and bilingual helper who makes picnics and ensures everything runs smoothly. Our holidays combine the great sites of antiquity with smaller places you would be unlikely to find on your own. We try to include country walks to sites, local food, and our accommodation is in hotels of character. Andante has been offering holidays since 1985 and carries around 300 passengers each year.'
Special interest holidays: Archaeology, art history tours

Anglo-Italian Study Tours
35 Murray Mews,
London NW1 9RH
Admin: 071-482 3767
Res: 071-482 3767
Fax: 071-916 7327
'We are a specialist company offering six day study tours in Tuscany. They are not run-of-the-mill tours – they do not include standing for hours in the crowded Uffizi. Instead we try to see buildings, sculpture, landscape and paintings as if discovering them through the eyes of earlier English travellers. Our house party holidays are based near Lucca, with accommodation in an elegantly restored ancient Tuscan farmhouse. A maximum of 14 guests enjoy local cuisine and wines. Days are spent discovering Romanesque and Renaissance art and architecture in local towns and villages.'
Special interest holidays: Art history tours

Arblaster & Clarke
Wine Tours
104 Church Road,
Steep, Petersfield GU32 2DP
Admin: 0730 266883
Res: 0730 266883
Fax: 0730 268620
ATOL: 2543
AITO
Credit cards: VISA ACCESS
'Established in November 1986, Arblaster & Clarke Wine Tours is an independent family run firm offering wine tours escorted by leading wine experts. Italy is ideal for wine touring – from the well known vineyards of Tuscany to lesser known regions in the North – around Verona for Soave and Valpolicella and

around Alba for the great wines of Barolo. These wine tours are designed for wine enthusiasts of all levels of knowledge. A special feature are meals at the cellars or the homes of the wine makers, giving an unique insight into a country that few holidays can offer. A further pleasure of wine touring in Italy is the cultural, gastronomic and musical delights with which this can be complemented, and we have combined many of these into the programme.'
Special interest holidays: Wine tours, Music holidays, Cooking holidays

Artscape Painting Holidays
Suite 4, Hamlet Court
Business Centre,
18 Hamlet Court Road,
Westcliff-on-Sea SS0 7LX
Admin: 0702 435990
Res: 0702 435990
Credit cards: VISA ACCESS
'Artscape offers a choice of 60 courses, each one carefully planned to suit the centre and with a course programme for artists with a range of interests and talents. We offer a choice of locations, tutors and courses. If you enjoy being with a certain tutor, you can join him or her at a different place each year. There is an extensive range of courses this year – modern and traditional, portrait and landscape for foundation and advanced students. Our painting groups are seldom more than 15, never more than 20. Non-painting partners are welcome.'
Special interest holidays: Painting and drawing holidays

Astons Coaches
4 Church Street,
Kempsey, Worcester WR5 3JG
Admin: 0905 821390
Res: 0905 821390
Fax: 0905 820850
'As a coaching company we have been trading for 63 years. It is a family run and family owned business. We provide a varied programme of sightseeing and multi-centre tours, beach holidays, short breaks and day trips to destinations home and abroad. Bonded by the Bus and Coach Council, these all-inclusive holidays incorporate a comprehensive package of excursions organised by the driver/courier, who stays with you throughout your holiday. Our Italian tours to Jesolo and Cavallino on the Venetian Riviera, are enhanced by a further team of staff who support the driver/couriers with an evening entertainment programme which includes spaghetti nights, pizza tasting nights, our own disco and cabaret and a B-B-Q party. Cavallino

offers a cheaper family-orientated holiday where staff are responsible for everything from re-pegging your tent to organising your excursions. Our three star hotels offer full-board and private beach facilities. Our excursion programme includes trips to Venice and surrounding islands, wine tasting, visits to traditional markets, a day trip to Lake Garda and a chance to experience open air opera at Verona.'
Special interest holidays: Coach holidays

At Home in Italy
87 Heathlee Road,
Blackheath, London SE3 9TS
Admin: 081-852 0069
Res: 081-852 0069
Diana Llewelyn Patt is a travel writer who has lived for long periods in Italy, France, Spain, Switzerland and the Greek Islands. She offers hotel and self-catering holidays in Tuscany, Umbria, the Gulf of Gaeta, Sardinia and the Sorrentine peninsula. 'I have slept and eaten in all the hotels I use. I have been operating for seven years and carry around 1000 people annually.'
Hotel holidays: Tuscany, Umbria, Rome and surrounding region, Naples and surrounding region, Sardinia

Auto Plan Holidays
Energy House, Lombard Street, Lichfield WS13 6DP
Admin: 0543 257777
Res: 0543 257777
Fax: 0543 419217
Credit cards: VISA ACCESS
'We offer a personal service for clients interested in self drive and fly drive holidays. We have been trading since 1984. There are only three employees and 65% of clients return each year. We have around 2000 clients annually and offer holidays in small hotels and apartments or villas. We feature the Lakes, Tuscany and the Dolomites. We include *en route* stopovers in our prices for motorists. We plan routes to our clients' requirements and we personally know well the areas and the accommodation we offer.'
Hotel holidays: Lakes, Tuscany
Self-catering holidays: Lakes, Tuscany

Beach Villas
8 Market Passage,
Cambridge CB2 3QR
Admin: 0223 311113
Res: 0223 311113
ABTA: 1415
ATOL: 2776
AITO
Credit cards: VISA ACCESS AMEX
Beach Villas has offered villa and apartment holidays for 27 years. 'We have developed a

special relationship with our villa owners and clients. Beach Villas has grown to become one of the largest privately owned travel companies in the UK. Each of our properties is chosen for its comfort, location and value for money, ranging from large villas with private pools to smaller studio apartments. All the properties featured within our programme are intimately known to us, and our staff have first hand knowledge of the resorts and properties.'
Self-catering holidays: Tuscany, Islands

Blackheath Wine Trails
13 Blackheath Village,
London SE3 9LA
Admin: 081-463 0012
Res: 081-463 0012
Fax: 081-463 0011
ABTA: 163
Credit cards: VISA ACCESS AMEX
'Blackheath Wine Trails has been trading for nine years and carries approximately 600 clients each year. As our name implies, we take the rather more relaxed routes through the vineyards, with plenty of time during our visits and tastings to obtain a great deal of technical information without making it a lecture tour – and you will linger over some memorable meals. You do not have to be a wine buff or indeed have any prior knowledge of wine to enjoy our trips. Tours average between 20 and 30 participants and appeal to all age groups. Single people are very welcome.'
Self-catering holidays: Tuscany
Special interest holidays: Wine tours, Cooking holidays

Bridgewater's Toscana
217 Monton Road, Monton,
Manchester M30 9PN
Admin: 061-787 8587
Res: 061-787 8587
Fax: 061-787 8896
ABTA: 0219
Credit cards: VISA ACCESS
'Bridgewater's Toscana specialises in summer lets of Tuscan properties and we occupy ourselves arranging several hundred individually tailored holidays for independent travellers each year. Our involvement with this lovely unspoiled region of Italy goes back to 1972, starting with Bellaglen Italian Villas in Marina di Pietrasanta and we are now accepted as part of the local scene. We choose each property because in our opinion it has an extra something a little out of the ordinary and must always offer good value for money, though not necessarily be the cheapest. The fact that the majority of our clients travel with us year after year and

recommend us to their friends, encourages us to believe it is a successful formula.'
Self-catering holidays: Tuscany

Brompton Travel
64 Richmond Road,
Kingston-upon-Thames
KT2 5EH
Admin: 081-549 3334
Res: 081-549 3334
Fax: 081-547 1160
ABTA: 17228
ATOL: 1039
'We are a small company which has been trading for 30 years. We carry over 300 people to Italy every year. We specialise in opera holidays.'
Special interest holidays: Music holidays

CV Travel
43 Cadogan Street, Chelsea,
London SW3 2PR
Admin: 071-581 0851
Res: 071-584 8803
Fax: 071-584 5229
ABTA: 23290
ATOL: 337
AITO
Credit cards: VISA ACCESS
CV Travel has been operating for 23 years and offers villa and hotel holidays throughout the Mediterranean, the Greek Islands of Corfu and Paxos, the Caribbean and the Indian Ocean. 'All our villas have swimming pools, many have a private tennis court

and also some of the larger houses have a cook/housekeeper in addition to maid service. The villas range in size from those suitable for just two people through to substantial villas offering spacious accommodation for large families or groups of friends. Our selection of hotels has been chosen either for their beautiful location and restaurant, or the variety of leisure and sporting facilities offered.'
Hotel holidays: Tuscany
Self-catering holidays: Umbria, Tuscany

Caravan & Camping Service
69 Westbourne Grove,
London W2 4UJ
Admin: 071-792 1944
Res: 071-792 1944
Fax: 071-792 1956
AITO
Credit cards: VISA ACCESS
'Caravan & Camping Service offers a pitch and ferry reservation service for campers and caravanners who wish to travel abroad. Arrangements are completely flexible – start any day, visit as many campsites as you wish and stay for any length of time. Our holidays are particularly suited to families looking for good value during the high season and couples who can travel in low season. We have over 14 years' experience of arranging

133

camping and caravanning holidays abroad, but are still a small company, able to offer personal service. Our advice and comprehensive travel pack is particularly appreciated by those travelling for the first time. Our sites are high quality, with a wide range of amenities and have been carefully selected. The sites on offer are in Cecina, Tuscany, Lake Maggiore, Lake Garda and on the Lido di Jesolo.'

Special interest holidays: Camping, Caravans and mobile homes

Carefree Italy
44 Central Parade, New
Addington, Croydon CR0 0JD
Admin: 0689 841900
Res: 0689 841900
Fax: 0689 841616
ABTA: 51021
Credit cards: VISA ACCESS
'We are a tour operator which has been in business since the early 70s, organising tailor made holidays worldwide. We decided to specialise in Italy and our first brochure was issued in 1991. We offer self-catering properties in Tuscany, Umbria, Marche and Lazio. All our properties are rigorously vetted. We expect to carry 2000 passengers for the current season.'
Self-catering holidays: Tuscany, Umbria

Citalia
Marco Polo House,
3-5 Lansdowne Road,
Croydon CR9 1LL
Admin: 081-680 5336
Res: 081-686 5533
Fax: 081-686 0328
ABTA: 17764
ATOL: 285
AITO
Credit cards: VISA ACCESS
AMEX DINERS
'Citalia began selling Italian holidays from the UK over 60 years ago and is the leading specialist tour operator to Italy. We are part of the CIT World Travel Group which itself is owned by Italian State Railways. We carry approximately 25,000 passengers annually to the parts of Italy most sought after by travellers – ie the cities of Rome, Florence, Venice and Verona, the Lakes and Mountains, Sorrento and the Amalfi Coast, Tuscany and Umbria, Sicily and Sardinia and the Tuscany coast. Through our tailor-made department we can offer all kinds of independent arrangements to most of Italy. We know Italy inside out and provide a high level of personal service both during the booking stage and at the point of delivery.'
Hotel holidays: Naples and surrounding region, Tuscany, Lakes, Sardinia, Sicily
Self-catering holidays: Venice

and the Veneto, Naples and surrounding region, Tuscany, Umbria, Lakes, Sicily

Club Med
106-110 Brompton Road,
London SW3 1JJ
Admin: 071-225 1066
Res: 071-581 1161
Fax: 071-589 6086
ABTA: 19685
ATOL: 1020
Credit cards: VISA ACCESS AMEX
'Club Med is a Public Limited Company which was founded in 1950. Over the last 43 years it has become the 10th largest international hotel chain in the world. Club Med offers holidays at all-inclusive prices in "villages" located in 32 countries worldwide. Nearly two million holidaymakers travel with Club Med each year (25,000 from the UK) of which 50% are families. The all-inclusive price represents return flights and transfers, accommodation, all sports and tuition, evening entertainment, children's clubs and travel insurance. We offer an enormous range of watersports, landsports and leisure activities for the whole family. An international team of staff ensure that all aspects of village life run smoothly. Creating a unique atmosphere in each village, they are instructors by day, table companions at mealtimes and entertainers by night. All villages have a similar layout which aims to provide all amenities within the Club Med complex: a reception/information centre, a shop, a boutique, a bank/bureau de change, an infirmary, restaurants, bars and a nightclub, children's clubs, a theatre and all the sports facilities. The children's clubs take charge of children between four months and 17 years, allowing parents to enjoy their holiday as adults, knowing their children are professionally supervised with a whole range of activities and sports organised for them depending on the age group.'
Special interest holidays: Club Holidays

Contiki Travel
Wells House,
15 Elmfield Road,
Bromley, Kent BR1 1LS
Admin: 081-290 6777
Res: 081-290 6422
Fax: 081-290 6569
ABTA: 20305
ATOL: 2689
AITO
Credit cards: VISA AMEX
'Contiki is a coach tour operator for the 18-35s. It has been operating for over 30 years with offices in 12 countries and 45,000 clients per annum worldwide. It offers tours

throughout Australia, New Zealand, America, Canada, Hawaii, Europe, Scandinavia, Great Britain, Egypt, the Greek Islands and Israel. Accommodation ranges from chateaux, manor houses, villas and gasthofs to top class hotels and country campsites. The luxury coaches are air conditioned and the young Contiki crew are enthusiastic and professionally trained."
Special interest holidays: Coach holidays

Continental Villas
3 Caxton Walk, Phoenix Street, London WC2H 8PW
Admin: 071-497 0444
Res: 071-497 0444
Fax: 071-379 5222
ABTA: 60919
AITO
Credit cards: VISA ACCESS
'Our company has 31 years of experience in renting luxury villas and apartments. We have a wide programme in Tuscany and Umbria and can tailor make any holiday to our clients' requirements.'
Self-catering holidays: Tuscany

Cosmosair
Tourama House,
17 homesdale road,
Bromley, Kent BR2 9LX
Admin: 061 480 9996
Res: 061 480 5799
Fax: 061 480 0833
ABTA: 23318
ATOL: 2275
Credit cards: VISA ACCESS
'Cosmos is part of a major, Swiss-owned, international travel organisation with interests worldwide. In the UK the group includes Avro plc, a large flight-only operator, and Monarch Airlines, one of the country's leading independent charter airlines. Overseas, the group owns Globus Gateway, the largest organisation of European coach touring holidays in the world, with a strong presence in the North American market. Established more than 30 years ago, Cosmos is one of the UK's leading and longest running tour operators and has been offering holidays to Italy since its inception across a range of products to suit every taste and budget. The Cosmos air and coach programmes together carry in excess of 500,000 passengers annually. Most areas of Italy are included in one or more of the different holiday brochures. Of special interest to the family market is Cosmos Sunlink, offering top value hotels and apartments on the Venetian Riviera where children can travel free or enjoy large reductions on the adult price as well as take advantage of the new Sooty club which offers supervised fun for two to 10-year-olds at

all Sunlink hotels. Cosmos also offers free local departures from over 290 pick up points throughout the UK.'

Hotel holidays: Lakes, Venice and the Veneto, Naples and surrounding region, All over Italy

Self-catering holidays: Venice and the Veneto

Special interest holidays: Coach holidays

Cresta Holidays

Cresta House,
32 Victoria Street,
Altrincham WA14 1ET
Admin: 061 926 8817
Res: 061 927 7000
Fax: 061 929 1114
ABTA: 23996
ATOL: 606
Credit cards: VISA ACCESS AMEX

'Cresta Holidays is one of the UK's leading city break specialists. We also offer holidays to France and Euro Disney in particular. We are fully bonded with ABTA and the CAA. We carried over 180,000 passengers on our 1993 programme. We launched a specialist Italian brochure last year. Although Cresta has featured the major Italian cities for many years, this was its first venture into other areas, including the Lakes, Tuscany, Umbria and the Neapolitan Riviera. The main feature of our programme is

flexibility – enabling clients to put together their own itinerary to any of the hotels, choosing either a fly-drive or a fly-rail option. There is also the facility to fly into one Italian airport and depart from another, giving much greater freedom. For example, fly into Milan, visit Lake Como and Verona then depart from Venice.'

Self-catering holidays: Tuscany
Special interest holidays: City breaks

Crestar Yacht Charters

Colette Court,
125 Sloane Street,
London SW1X 9AU
Admin: 071-730 9962
Res: 071-730 9962
Fax: 071-824 8691
Credit cards: AMEX

'Crestar Yacht Charters was established over a decade ago and is one of the leading companies specialising in the chartering of luxury private yachts with professional uniformed crews. It offers a wide selection of both motor and sailing yachts from 80ft to over 200 ft. Yachts are personally inspected on an annual basis and the company's charter consultants are both highly knowledgeable and helpful. All charters are tailor-made to suit individual requirements. Yachts are available throughout Italian

waters, including San Remo, Portofino, Elba, Capri, the Amalfi Coast and Sardinia. An expensive but undoubtedly extremely exclusive way to explore Italy's superb coastal regions.'
Special interest holidays: Sailing

DA Tours
Williamton House,
Low Causeway,
Culross, Fife KY12 8HL
Admin: 0383 881700
Res: 0383 881700
Fax: 0383 881501
ABTA: 76264
Credit cards: VISA ACCESS
'We are a private company specialising in middle-priced, fully inclusive coach holidays. We have traded successfully for 12 years, carrying up to 10,000 clients per year. Italian destinations include the Lakes, Tuscany, Sorrento and the classical cities.'
Special interest holidays: Coach holidays

Enterprise
Owners Abroad House,
Peel Cross Road, Salford,
Manchester M5 2AN
Admin: 061-745 4633
Res: 061-745 7000
Fax: 061-745 4533
ABTA: 68342
ATOL: 230
Credit cards: VISA ACCESS
Enterprise is part of the

Owners Abroad Group, Britain's second largest holiday company. It has its own airline – Air 2000 – which handles most of its holiday flights. In Italy it offers hotel holidays to the Neapolitan Riviera.
Hotel holidays: Naples and surrounding region

Euro-Academy
77a George Street,
Croydon, Surrey CR0 1LD
Admin: 081-680 4618
Res: 081-686 2363
Fax: 081-681 8850
Credit cards: VISA ACCESS AMEX
'Euro Academy has been arranging language courses for 23 years. It is a small independent operator providing a wide range of courses. Effective language learning is a partnership between the school, the teacher and the student – we monitor this partnership carefully. In Italy we offer four destinations: Florence, Rome, Siena and Milan. Our Italian courses operate all year for all levels and all ages (18 years and over). We arrange intensive tuition in small groups in all four destinations from two weeks. In Florence it is possible to combine language tuition and Art History. We provide one to one crash courses for one week in the

Business Class brochure for executives. Lunchtime with the teacher may provide the opportunity to simulate a business lunch or simply serve as a pleasant way to enjoy food in a relaxed atmosphere while practising Italian. At the Art Institute in Florence, there is the opportunity to learn drawing or painting in four week workshops in May, June or July – there is no prerequisite for admission.'
Special interest holidays: Language learning

EuroSites
Wavell House,
Holcombe Road, Helmshore,
Rossendale BB4 4NB
Admin: 0706 830888
Res: 0706 830888
Fax: 0706 830248
Credit cards: VISA ACCESS
EuroSites is part of the Airtours Group. It offers camping and mobile home holidays throughout Europe. In Italy it offers three locations: Lake Garda, Lido di Jesolo and the Tuscan coast.
Special interest holidays: Camping

Eurocamp Travel Ltd
Canute Court, Toft Road,
Knutsford WA16 0NL
Admin: 0565 650022
Res: 0565 626262
Fax: 0565 654930

ABTA: 70677
AITO
Credit cards: VISA ACCESS
'Eurocamp has been trading for 21 years. We offer self-drive camping and mobile home holidays throughout Europe. Accommodation is in luxury six berth ready-erected tents or eight berth mobile homes. Holidays are individually tailored to each customer's requirements – you can depart on any day of the week and stay for any length of time (subject to a three night minimum). Customers can choose from a wide variety of ferry crossings. We also offer a Motorail service which includes services from Calais to Bologna, Livorno, Milan and Rome. Eurocamp Travel is part of the Eurocamp Group which is listed on the stock market, and in 1993 carried in the region of 125,000 holidaymakers. We offer 270 campsites in 13 European countries. We offer 36 Italian campsites in Tuscany, Umbria, Campania, Italian Lakes, Dolomites, Venice area and Trieste.'
Special interest holidays: Camping

Eurovillas
36 East Street,
Coggleshall, Essex CO6 1SH
Admin: 0376 561156
Res: 0376 561156

Fax: 0376 583902

'Eurovillas is currently a part-nership, and has been an established self-catering company for some 30 years. We were founder members of the National Villa Association when self-catering holidays were in their infancy. We are not part of a large organisa-tion and pride ourselves on our independence and personal service. All proper-ties let by us are personally inspected by ourselves and, in virtually all cases, we work directly with the owner of the apartment/villa. Although we are a small organisation, carrying well under 1000 people annually, many of our clients are repeat customers who rely on our tailoring to their requirements. The areas we cover in Italy are those in and around Lucca (both inside the walled city and in the surrounding countryside) and in the areas of Arezzo/ Sansepolcro/Cortona. We also have apartments in and around Bardolino on Lake Garda. Our knowledge of the regions we cover is extensive and many places we offer are only given by the owners to us because they know and trust our operation.'

Self-catering holidays: Lakes, Tuscany

Excelsior Holidays
22 Sea Road,
Bournemouth BH5 1DD
Admin: 0202 309555
Res: 0202 309733
Fax: 0202 391744
ABTA: 27728
Credit cards: VISA ACCESS

'We are a privately-owned coach holiday company which has been family-owned since the 1920s. We carry up to 35,000 people annually in our fleet of 50 coaches. Our holidays to Italy include the lakes and mountains, Tuscany, the Bay of Naples and a special tour to Venice and Rome.'

Special interest holidays: Coach holidays

Exodus
9 Weir Road,
London SW17 0LT
Admin: 081-675 5550
Res: 081-675 5550
Fax: 081-673 0779
ATOL: 2582
AITO
Credit cards: VISA ACCESS AMEX

'Exodus has been established for more than 20 years as an operator offering walking and adventure holidays. The directors of Exodus today have been with the company since its conception in 1973. In 1979, Exodus introduced its walking programme and later in 1982, a range of adventure

trips. During that time the company has developed programmes to meet the demands of those who want more out of their holiday than sun and sea, but do not always have the time for longer expeditions.'
Special interest holidays: Walking and trekking, adventure holidays

Explore Worldwide
1 Frederick Street,
Aldershot, Hants GU11 1LQ
Admin: 0252 319448
Res: 0252 319448
Fax: 0252 343170
ATOL: 2595
AITO
Credit cards: VISA ACCESS
Explore was formed in 1981 and offers small group exploratory holidays. In 1992 over 10,000 people travelled with the company. 'Our approach from the start has been to travel in small groups, causing as little environmental damage and cultural disturbance as possible. We achieve this mainly by utilising local resources and services. This year our brochure contains over 160 original adventure programmes in more than 70 countries.' In Italy the company offers volcano hiking in Sicily and walking through Tuscany.
Special interest holidays:

Walking and trekking, Adventure holidays

Fine Art Travel
15 Savile Row,
London W1X 1AE
Admin: 071-437 8553
Res: 071-437 8553
Fax: 071-437 1733
Fine Art Travel is a specialist company offering art history holidays to Rome, Ravenna, Urbino and Venice. Among its directors it lists Sir Hugh Casson.
Special interest holidays: Art history tours

Fourwinds Holidays
Bearland House, Longsmith Street, Gloucester GL1 2HL
Admin: 0452 524151
Res: 0452 527656
Fax: 0452 419312
ABTA: 23360
ATOL: 1638
Credit cards: VISA ACCESS AMEX DINERS
'Cotswold Fourwinds has been trading for 13 years, based in the Gloucester area. It is a predominantly European coaching tour operator, but in the last few years it has organised a number of long-haul products, for example, West Coast USA, Thailand and Canada. The company forms part of Cannon Street Investments plc and it carries approximately 55,000 passengers annually. Cotswold Four-

winds has operated two main programmes to Italy over a couple of years: an Italian Lakes and Dolomites tour based in Levico and an Italian Riviera trip based in Alassio.'
Special interest holidays: Coach holidays

Fresco Cycling
69-71 Banbury Road,
Oxford OX2 6PE
Admin: 0865 310399
Res: 0865 310399
Fax: 0865 310299
ATOL: 2618
AITO
Credit cards: VISA ACCESS
'Fresco Cycling is part of the Alternative Travel Group (founded in 1979). It offers independent journeys by bicycle through the most beautiful and interesting parts of Europe. Go when you like, cycle as far as you like each day, and spend as long as you like at each place *en route*. You can tailor the cost to your budget by selecting from various grades of accommo- dation: rooms in village houses to premier de-luxe. Our representative welcomes you on arrival, fits you with a newly serviced all-terrain bicycle and looks after all your arrangements and trans- ports your luggage while you are cycling.'
Special interest holidays: Cycling holidays

Gordon Overland
76 Croft Road,
Carlisle CA3 9AG
Admin: 0228 26795
Res: 0228 26795
'We have been trading for a decade. We are not part of any larger group. We carry only a few hundred people annually. We feature Tuscany, Umbria, Rome and Lombardy but can make suitable arrangements for families and small groups anywhere in Italy. Our service is that of a consultancy and is therefore very personal. Our connections in Italy make our products unique. As a consul- tancy we try to obtain what travellers and holidaymakers want at a price they think is reasonable. Over the past year we have made arrangements for groups as diverse as seven Franciscan friars seeking accommodation in Florence to a couple wanting to buy a flat in Rome. Other groups have included a party of university lecturers taking a break on Ischia in stylish surroundings, property brokers in Perugia in a palace and families in Rome, Viareggio and on Ischia. For 1994 we have a special project to create 'U3A Eden-Iseo' – the first ever residential University of the Third Age, offering a range of mildly academic courses based in hotels situated beside Lake Iseo using the resources to

be found in Lombardy and Friuli-Venezia to create a unique institution. The project aims to provide adult education in Italy at a price unobtainable from any other source.'

Hotel holidays: All over Italy

Self-catering holidays: All over Italy

Special interest holidays: Language learning, Study holidays, Walking and trekking, Horseriding

HF Walking Holidays
Imperial House,
Edgware Road,
London NW9 5AL
Admin: 081-905 9556
Res: 081-905 9558
Fax: 081-205 0506
ATOL: 710
Credit cards: VISA ACCESS

'HF Holidays has over 80 years' experience and today is the world leader in walking and special interest holidays. In the UK, HF own 19 country house hotels, mostly located in areas of outstanding natural beauty. Each year 30,000 people take their holidays with HF – 99% of whom say they enjoyed their holiday so much they will return to take another. HF also offer walking holidays throughout Europe and further afield. European destinations include Austria, France, Slovenia, Switzerland, Malta, Portugal, Spain, Greece, Holland and Italy. In Italy, destinations include Sorrento and the Bay of Naples in Spring, and Tuscany and Lake Garda in the summer. Our holidays give a unique daily choice of walks led by trained and experienced HF leaders. This choice means you can always select a walk which suits your own ability. Our hotels are small, often family run and renowned for beautiful surroundings.'

Special interest holidays: Walking and trekking

HPS Hotels Direct
823-825 High Road,
Finchley, London N12 8UB
Admin: 081-446 0126
Res: 081-446 0126
Fax: 081-446 0196
Credit cards: VISA ACCESS AMEX DINERS

'HPS represents over 2000 hotels and self-catering properties worldwide. With over 30 years' experience in the travel industry, we operate a reservations service for independent travellers, business people and groups. Our reservations service is free, our rates are competitive and we always have hotels on special offer or discount. One phone call gives you: a range of properties, instant room availability, the flexibility to design your own itinerary, no

obligatory packages and access to advice and recommendations.'
Hotel holidays: All over Italy

Haven Europe
Northney Marina,
Northney Road,
Hayling Island,
Hants PO11 0NH
Admin: 0705 466111
Res: 0705 466111
ABTA: 30627
Credit cards: VISA ACCESS
Haven offer self-drive camping and mobile home holidays in France, Spain and Italy. It is part of The Rank Organisation plc and has been trading for 20 years.
Special interest holidays: Camping

Holts' Battlefield Tours
Golden Key Building,
15 Market Street, Sandwich,
Kent CT13 9DA
Admin: 0304 612248
Res: 0304 612248
Fax: 0304 614930
ATOL: 2846
AITO
'Major and Mrs Holt's Battlefield Tours started in 1977 as a result of The Military Book Society selecting one of their books featuring The First World War, and then asking the Holts to conduct tours of the battlefields of The Somme and Ypres Salient for their readers. This was the begin-ning of a series of subsequent tours featuring military history all over the world. In December 1992, Tonie and Valmai Holt retired from touring and sold the company to a specialist tour group – Green Fields Leisure – with other branches specialising in horse racing and Grand Prix racing. We carry 3000-3500 people each year and always stay in good hotels (in Italy three and four star) and use reliable coach companies and airlines. In 1994 we will be taking groups to the 50th Annniversary of The Battles of Cassino and The Anzio Salient and to the Ravenna-Lake Comacchio area for the study of the breaking of the 'Gothic Line' in Northern Italy in 1944-45. Each of our tours is led by experienced guides, two to each group, and all that the traveller has to buy is lunch on tour. Care and good value for money is our principal aim!'
Special interest holidays: Battlefield Tours

Hoseasons Holidays Abroad
Sunway House,
Lowestoft, Suffolk NR32 2LW
Admin: 0502 500505
Res: 0502 500555
Fax: 0502 500532
ABTA: 3557
ATOL: 2290

Credit cards: VISA ACCESS
'Hoseason's Holidays is a booking agent for boating holidays and for the renting of holiday homes. The company celebrates its 50th anniversary in 1994. Whilst the main core of the business is holidays in the UK, since 1984 the company has operated a growing holidays abroad programme, which involves boating holidays in France and Holland and holiday homes in France, Holland, Germany, Belgium, Italy and Northern Spain. The holidays abroad programme carries around 45,000 passengers per year including about 700 to Italy. Whilst the Italian programme is small we expect to expand it in the years ahead. The accommodation in Italy is mainly centred in the south of Tuscany around the villages of Roccastrada and Sassofortino, together with a few coastal houses near Castiglione della Pescaia. All our homes are checked each year. '
Self-catering holidays: Tuscany

Ilios Island Holidays
18 Market Square, Horsham,
West Sussex RH12 1EU
Admin: 0403 259788
Res: 0403 259788
Fax: 0403 211699
ABTA: 76635
ATOL: 1452
AITO

Credit cards: VISA ACCESS
'Ilios Island Holidays has been trading as an independent tour operator since 1980 and is not associated with either a larger tour operator or other organisation. The company, which carries approximately 2500 passengers annually, maintains an excellent rapport with its clients. Our Italian Collection includes farmhouses with private pools set mostly in the countryside of Tuscany, Umbria, the Marche, Abruzzo and Liguria. All our properties are carefully selected by us personally, thus enabling us to offer our clients the first hand information which we feel so vital when choosing their holiday. Each holiday is tailor made to suit individual requirements and the very personal service offered by the company ensures a high level of repeat business and recommendations.'
Self-catering holidays: Tuscany, Umbria, Italian Riviera, Abruzzo, Marche, Rome and surrounding region, Venice and the Veneto

Inntravel
The Old Station,
Helmsley, York YO6 5BZ
Admin: 0439 71111
Res: 0439 71111
Fax: 0439 71070
ATOL: 2644

AITO
Credit cards: VISA ACCESS
'Inntravel is a specialist in independent travel and has been established for nine years. The company offers holidays in the unspoilt places of Norway, France, Switzerland and the South Tyrol of Italy. It picks out authentic villages in hills and mountains and links together discovery hotels, active journeys and cottages. It is possible to combine different countries and travel by air, car, boat or train. Two thirds of the company's business comes from repeat bookings and recommended friends.'
Hotel holidays: Dolomites
Special interest holidays: Walking and trekking

Insight Holidays
6 Gareloch Road,
Port Glasgow PA14 5XH
Admin: 0475 742366
Res: 0800 393 393
Fax: 0475 742073
ABTA: 18254
ATOL: 1513
AITO
Credit cards: VISA ACCESS
Insight offer escorted coach touring holidays all over Europe. 'We'll show you the sights you always wanted to see as well as others you never knew existed. You'll meet and mingle with people, share their history, art and culture – and sample their cuisine. Our itineraries provide two and three night stops so you have the time to do the things you want and we stay in hotels which are mostly first class or better, well located in the cities and close to major scenic attractions.'
Special interest holidays: Coach holidays

Interhome
383 Richmond Road,
Twickenham TW1 2EF
Admin: 081-891 1294
Res: 081-891 1294
Fax: 081-891 5331
ABTA: 3684
Credit cards: VISA ACCESS
'Interhome has been letting out holiday homes since 1965. It is part of the Swiss Hotelplan Group. Over the years it has built up a large selection of privately owned houses and apartments for rent throughout Europe. At the last count it was offering a choice of over 20,000 properties of all sizes and price ranges. There are 3000 holiday homes for rent throughout Italy. The majority of these are situated in the most popular holiday areas of Tuscany and Liguria. There are small apartments for two people and large houses for up to 10 people.'
Self-catering holidays: All over Italy

International Chapters

102 St John's Wood Terrace,
London NW8 6PL
Admin: 071-722 9560
Res: 071-722 9560
Fax: 071-722 9140
Credit cards: VISA ACCESS
AMEX DINERS

'International Chapters is an independent company and has been trading for 10 years. We carry approximately 4000 people annually to Italy. We cover mainly Tuscany and Umbria, but also have properties to rent in the Veneto, Italian Lakes, Lazio, Apulia, Calabria, Sicily and Sardinia. We also have a programme of Italian city apartments – mainly in central Venice, and a small selection in Florence and Rome. We also act as UK representatives for two Tuscany-based companies: Tuscan Enterprises and Cuendet. Tuscan Enterprises offers over 100 properties in the Chianti area – ranging from apartments to large villas, most with sole or shared use of a swimming pool. Prices range from £270 to £2000 per property, per week. Cuendet offers over 1000 properties mainly in Tuscany and Umbria, but also a good selection in the Veneto, Lazio, Apulia, Calabria, Sicily, Elba and Sardinia. Prices range from £150 to £2000 per property, per week.'

Self-catering holidays: Tuscany, Umbria, Venice and the Veneto, Florence, Rome and surrounding region

International Services USA Inc

Via Del Babuino, 79, 00187
Rome, Italy
Admin: 06/3600-0018/0019
Res: 06/3600-0018/0019
Fax: 06/3600-0037

'International Services is an American firm which has been in the rental business for 10 years. We service an international clientele of roughly 400 people annually. We have offices in Rome, London and the USA. We represent properties in every province of Italy – all the major cities as well as the islands. Our holidays are particularly special because our rentals are rarely of the commercial type. They are homes often used by the owners and therefore well maintained, furnished and decorated in a style characteristic to the area.'

Self-catering holidays: All over Italy

Invitation to Tuscany

PO Box 2 TSB House, Le Truchot, St Peter Port, Guernsey GY1 3AA
Admin: 061-775 6637
Res: 061-775 6637
Fax: 021 428 1476
Credit cards: VISA

'Invitation to Tuscany is a small company, arranging self-catering holidays for over 200 people each year in central Tuscany, one of the most beautiful and civilised places in the world. Based in Guernsey, the Company uses three agents, two in Britain and one in North America. They are people who know the properties and the area well and can discuss them personally with customers. In addition, an English, bi-lingual representative lives permanently in Tuscany. Properties are privately-owned and carefully chosen to provide an appropriate backdrop in this richly diverse and rewarding country. From romantic cottages for two to large villas with swimming pools and tennis courts for great family holidays, all the properties are in beautiful positions – in picturesque countryside or in evocative hill villages within easy reach of the most fascinating towns in Tuscany. Holidays are special occasions and ever since it started in the late '70s, Invitation to Tuscany has built its business on its reputation for personal, reliable service. The company arranges ferry crossings, Motorail and car hire and will recommend bonded flight agents. Every customer is treated with equal importance whether they want a week in the simplest cottage or a month in the most expensive villa.'
Self-catering holidays: Tuscany

Italberghi
35 Bimport, Shaftesbury,
Dorset SP7 8AX
Admin: 0747 55855
Res: 0747 55855
Fax: 0747 51207
Credit cards: VISA ACCESS
'We are a hotel booking service which offers accommodation in cities, Tuscany and on the Lakes. During the last 24 years, we have got to know the hoteliers and hotels we use quite well. Our aim is always to provide accommodation in hotels which are conveniently situated, clean, adequately comfortable and small enough to be run on a personal basis. Most are owner-managed. They are not the cheapest available but do represent value for money. We inspect them as often as we can which usually means once a year.'
Hotel holidays: All over Italy

Italian Cookery Weeks
PO Box 2482,
London NW10 1HW
Admin: 081-208 0112
Res: 081-208 0112
Fax: 071-401 8763
ATOL: 173
Credit cards: VISA ACCESS

'Italian Cookery Weeks is the name of a gourmet holiday in two of the most beautiful parts of Italy: Umbria and Apulia – where guests will learn to master the secrets of traditional regional cooking. The tuition and accommodation is located in lovely old buildings on both the ancient farm estates, with all the bedrooms having a bathroom. The facilities include a swimming pool and a self-catering kitchen. During the week, guests are taken to the local market and to explore the historic towns of Assisi, Todi, Perugia or in the south Lecce, Alberobello and the Roman fisherman village of Monopoli. Our holidays have been operating since 1991 and are managed by Susanna Gelmetti who has appeared several times on BBC cookery programmes and until recently was the chef at London's Accademia Italiana delle Arti in Knightsbridge. The atmosphere is very friendly and guests return year after year, and it is definitely the most authentic Italian experience: nocturnal outings to the hot springs of Saturnia under a full moon, a barbecue of fish on the beach or truffle hunting with dogs in the woods near Orvieto very early in the morning. The courses run weekly from May to September.
Special interest holidays: Cooking holidays

Italian Escapades
227 Shepherds Bush Road,
London W6 7AS
Admin: 081-748 4999
Res: 081-748 2661
Fax: 081-563 0480
ABTA: 97275
ATOL: 2398
AITO
Credit cards: VISA ACCESS AMEX DINERS
'Italian Escapades has been trading for seven years and is part of the Air Travel Group which forms part of the leisure division of The Granada Group plc. It carries 18,000 people annually. Destinations featured include the Neapolitan Riviera, the Tuscany coast, Venice, Elba, Sicily, the Lakes and Dolomites, Tuscany, Umbria, the Veneto and 11 cities. It offers flexible holidays that you can design yourself straight from the brochure. You can choose from one night to several weeks and mix and match as many destinations as you wish.'
Hotel holidays: Naples and surrounding region, Tuscany, Sardinia, Islands, Sicily, Lakes, Umbria
Self-catering holidays: Naples and surrounding region, Tuscany

Special interest holidays: City breaks, Golfing holidays, Tennis

Italiatour
205 Holland Park Avenue,
London W11 4XB
Admin: 071-371 1114
Res: 071-371 1114
Fax: 071-602 6172
ATOL: 2485
AITO
Credit cards: VISA ACCESS AMEX DINERS
Italiatour is part of the Alitalia Group. It offers tailor-made holidays to Italy: city breaks, beach and lake resorts, multi-centre holidays, coach tours, self-catering holidays and music holidays.
Hotel holidays: All over Italy
Self-catering holidays: Tuscany, Umbria
Special interest holidays: City breaks, Coach holidays

Kirker Holidays
3 New Concordia Wharf,
Mill Street, London SE1 2BB
Admin: 071-231 3333
Res: 071-231 3333
Fax: 071-231 4771
ABTA: 38012
ATOL: 2450
AITO
Credit cards: VISA ACCESS AMEX
'Kirker Holidays is an independent company, founded in 1986 with the intention of offering quality holidays in

European cities. The keynote is flexibility: any flight, any airport, any duration, any city or combination of cities, any hotel. We include private transfers for all our arrivals direct from airport to hotel (water taxis in Venice, private cars or taxis elsewhere). Hotels tend to be smaller, more characterful properties, usually family owned and with a very high standard of furnishings and service – even in our more popular two star hotels. Last year 15,000 clients chose to travel with Kirker. Italian destinations include Venice, Florence, Rome, Bologna, Milan, Verona and Sorrento. However, any itinerary – including two or three centre holidays – can be arranged to include any hotel in any part of the country. Clients may travel out to one airport and back from another. Internal travel in Italy is by hired car or 1st class rail. All our holidays are effectively tailor-made, with immediate quotations on request.'
Special interest holidays: City breaks

La Bella Toscana
119 Lynton Road,
Harrow, Middx HA2 9NJ
Admin: 081-422 9218
Res: 081-422 9218
Fax: 081-869 1035

'La Bella Toscana is an estate agency run by myself, Gaynor Powell, and my Italian husband from our home and office in San Gimignano. For nearly 10 years we have been specialising in renting properties in San Gimignano itself and the magnificent surrounding countryside. All the villas, apartments and farmhouses are owned by local people who care about them and look after them well. They are visited by us regularly and are also well known to our agent in England, Maureen Ruck. All our visitors are received by us personally and given a pack of information including maps of the local area. To ensure that everyone has an enjoyable stay we are always available to give help and further information.'

Self-catering holidays: Tuscany

Liaisons Abroad

Nightingale House,
1-7 Fulham High Street,
London SW6 3JH
Admin: 071-371 8227
Res: 071-384 1122
Fax: 071-371 0647

'Liaisons Abroad started in April 1990 as an hotel sales and marketing agency, representing hotels based in Italy. We have since grown enormously in our range of services though still keeping to a small size operation which suits our tailor-made holiday programme. We provide land arrangements only and carry an average of 10,000 passengers a year. We have incorporated other countries and enlarged our portfolio to include cycling holidays, culture courses and opera holidays. Between hotel representation and the reservation of opera tickets we cover all regions of Italy, mainly the art cities and seaside resorts. For our opera holidays, we take reservations based on individual needs, with no restrictions on attendance, date or type of ticket, making it as easy to see performances abroad as it is for any national venue.'

Hotel holidays: All over Italy
Special interest holidays: Music holidays, Cycling holidays, Painting and drawing holidays

Long Travel

The Steps, All Stretton,
Shropshire SY6 6HG
Admin: 0694 722193
Res: 0694 722193
Fax: 0694 724291
Credit cards: VISA ACCESS

'Husband and wife team, Ray and Annie Long, make up the small family-run company, which operates from home and calls itself Long Travel. As specialists in Southern Italy, we search long and hard

to find the right blend of qualities for our clients – new ones and a long list of repeat clients, some of whom have been travelling with us since we started five years ago. We know all of our properties personally, and we will honestly answer any questions our clients may have and do our best to match clients to the destination most suited to them. Our chosen areas offer something different from other rather anglicised parts of Italy further north. We offer Apulia, Calabria and Sicily. We find all the nooks and crannies of undiscovered Italy and share our discoveries with the 600 clients who travel with us each year.'
Hotel holidays: Sicily
Self-catering holidays: Apulia, Calabria, Sicily

Made to Measure Holidays
43 East Street,
Chichester PO19 1HX
Admin: 0243 533333
Res: 0243 533333
Fax: 0243 778431
ABTA: 91921
ATOL: 1006
Credit cards: VISA ACCESS
'Made to Measure Holidays has been established for 20 years and is still a totally independent, family-owned company. Each year it carries 3000 customers abroad. It specialises in custom-made itineraries to exclusive hotels in Italy as well as other countries in Europe. Destinations include Venice, Florence, Siena, Rome, Milan and a handful of hotels on the sea in such places as as Porto, Ercole, Portofino, Sicily and Sardinia. Holiday durations can be from two to 30 nights, by air or self-drive. Made to Measure's brochure entitled "Romantic Escapes" captivates the imagination of people with a particular celebration in mind – maybe a wedding anniversary or a special birthday, or even a honeymoon. The hotels have been chosen for their combination of the five "C"s: charm, character, calm, courtesy and cuisine.'
Special interest holidays: City breaks

Magic of Italy
227 Shepherds Bush Road,
London W6 7AS
Admin: 081-748 4999
Res: 081-748 7575
Fax: 081-748 6381
ABTA: 97275
ATOL: 2398
AITO
Credit cards: VISA ACCESS AMEX
'The Magic of Italy has been trading for 20 years and is part of the Air Travel Group which forms part of the

leisure division of The Granada Group plc. We carry over 22,000 people annually. Our programme features Tuscany, Umbria, the Neapolitan Riviera, Sardinia, Sicily, Tuscan coastal resorts, Liguria, Puglia, the Lakes, Venice Lido, Veneto, Verona, Venice, Rome and Florence. Our holidays are for individuals who like to avoid mass tourism. All our hotels and villas are hand-picked. We pride ourselves on our service from reservations, through to in-flight service and our overseas representatives. Our team in the UK are extremely knowledgeable and experienced about Italy.'

Hotel holidays: All over Italy
Self-catering holidays: Tuscany, Umbria, Naples and surrounding region, Sicily, Puglia, Sardinia, Lakes, Venice and the Veneto
Special interest holidays: City breaks, Painting and drawing holidays

Mark Warner
20 Kensington Church Street, London W8 4EP
Admin: 071-937 9281
Res: 071-938 1851
Fax: 071-938 3861
ABTA: 20358
ATOL: 1176
Credit cards: VISA ACCESS
'Mark Warner is a specialist independent tour operator which has been trading for 17 years. It operates Winter Ski and Summer Beach Clubs programmes with free watersports. It carries around 20,000 passengers annually. The ski programme features the Clubhotel Telecabine in the Dolonne area of Courmayeur. This club is ideal for families with a full seven day crèche and childminding service available for children from six months to 12 years. Accommodation is in rooms with ensuite facilities, on a half-board basis plus a free seven day ski hosting service. During the summer, Mark Warner features the Club Punta Licosa located on the Tyrrhenian coast of southern Italy, between the Gulf of Salerno and Policastro. Accommodation is in rooms with ensuite facilities on a full-board basis, with free wine served during lunch and evening meal. Free waterskiing, windsurfing and dinghy sailing with tuition is available. A free crèche service for two-to-five-year-olds and a programme of activities for six-to-12-year-olds is featured. Other activities at the club include tennis, volleyball and aerobics. There is also a swimming pool.'
Special interest holidays: Club Holidays, Skiing

Martin Randall Travel
10 Barley Mow Passage,
Chiswick, London W4 4PH
Admin: 081-742 3355
Res: 081-742 3355
Fax: 081-742 1066
ABTA: 16070
ATOL: 1585
AITO
Credit cards: VISA ACCESS
Martin Randall Travel is a specialist operator offering escorted art, architecture, archaeology and music tours.
Special interest holidays: Music holidays, Art & Architecture Tours, Wine tours

Owners Abroad Travel
2nd Floor, Astral Towers,
Betts Way, Crawley West
Sussex RH10 2GX
Admin: 0293 554466
Res: 0293 554455
ATOL: 2600
Credit cards: VISA ACCESS
Tjaereborg, Martin Rooks, Sunfare and Timsway form the direct sell arm of the Owner's Abroad Group. They carry approximately 350,000 clients annually.
Hotel holidays: Lakes, Naples and surrounding region

Page & Moy
136-140 London Road,
Leicester LE2 1EN
Admin: 0533 542000
Res: 0533 524433
Fax: 0533 524124
ABTA: 47026
ATOL: 133
Credit cards: VISA ACCESS
'Page & Moy has been operating for over 30 years and was one of the founder members of ABTA. We offer an extensive holiday programme to Italy where primarily we organise two-centre tours. All groups have an escort and typically number 35 people. The principal areas covered are Tuscany, Umbria and Abruzzo including the cities of Florence, Venice and Rome. We are also a major operator to the Verona Opera Festival. Each year we carry over 12,000 passengers to Italy.'
Hotel holidays: Tuscany, Umbria, Naples and surrounding region, Lakes
Special interest holidays: Wine tours, Archaeology, Art & Architecture Tours, Music holidays

Portland Holidays
218 Great Portland Street,
London W1N 5HG
Admin: 071-388 5111
Res: 071-388 5111
ABTA: 5217
ATOL: 2524
Credit cards: VISA ACCESS
Portland is the direct sell arm of Thomson Holidays. It offers holidays throughout Europe, Egypt, Florida, Jamaica and the Dominican

Republic. In Italy its destination is Lake Garda.
Hotel holidays: Lakes

Premier Italy
Crystal House,
The Courtyard,
Arlington Road,
Surbiton KT6 6BW
Admin: 081-390 8033
Res: 081-390 5554
Fax: 081-390 6378
ABTA: 23816
ATOL: 1664
Credit cards: VISA ACCESS
'Premier Italy is part of Crystal Holidays and was launched on 26 October 1993. Crystal is in its 13th year of trading. It forecasts carrying 10,000 people this year to Italy. Destinations featured are Tuscany, Umbria, Lake Garda, the Neapolitan Riviera, Sicily, Florence, Rome and Venice. Departures are from Gatwick, Heathrow, Stansted, Luton, Manchester, Glasgow, Birmingham and Bristol. We offer accommodation-only prices for villas and hotels if clients wish it and also feature mix and match holidays where an unlimited choice of destinations is possible.'
Hotel holidays: All over Italy
Self-catering holidays: Tuscany
Special interest holidays: Coach holidays

Prospect Music and Art Tours
454-458 Chiswick High Road,
London W4 5TT
Admin: 081-995 2151
Res: 081-995 2151
Fax: 081-742 1969
ATOL: 2719
Credit cards: VISA ACCESS
Founded in 1982, Prospect specialises in art history and music tours. 'Following their great popularity in 1993, we are continuing our programme of partly-guided Cultural Weekends and Short Breaks. We use the same hotels, scheduled flights and travel arrangements as our fully-guided tours, and experienced Prospect guides will help to make the weekend interesting and memorable by accompanying a walk, an excursion, or other visit. Only part of the weekend is structured, allowing plenty of time for independent exploration.'
Destinations in Italy include Florence, Venice and Rome.
Special interest holidays: Art history tours

Ramblers Holidays
Box 43,
Welwyn Garden AL8 6PQ
Admin: 0707 331133
Res: 0707 331133
Fax: 0707 333276
ABTA: 50940
ATOL: 990
Credit cards: VISA ACCESS

'Ramblers Holidays was formed in 1946 to operate walking holidays and has done so ever since; and now does so all over the world. The main programmes are in the Alpine and hill countries of Europe. All holidays are graded from quite easy (D grade) to very tough (A grade) and are led either by a Ramblers' leader or a professional guide. Most tours include at least half pension and comprise parties of 15 to 20 people plus leader. The majority of holidays use scheduled or charter flights from London, several holidays include options for flying from Manchester. Accommodation is generally in two star hotels, sometimes in three, very rarely in one star, nearly always in rooms with private facilities. There are several tougher tours which use mountain hut accommodation which is much more basic. Each holiday, and there are 114 different holidays in the '94 brochure, clearly shows the type of accommodation used. Any profits made during the year are either ploughed into the Ramblers Association to progress their work in the British countryside, or used for other good deeds, one of which has included building a water pipeline, school and medical centre in the Annapurnon village of Ghonepani in Nepal. Over the years we have learned that it's not just the holiday which makes a Ramblers trip so enjoyable but the small parties of like-minded people who participate.'
Special interest holidays: Walking and trekking

Room Service
42 Riding House Street,
London W1P 7PL
Admin: 071-636 6888
Res: 071-636 6888
Fax: 071-636 6002
'Room Service is a new company, trading since 1992, which aims to offer an efficient, yet friendly, booking service for accommodation in Italy. We are totally independent, and as such we are free to sell any hotel that meets our standards. Over 2500 people used our services during 1993 to reserve rooms at small hotels and pensioni throughout Italy. The most popular destinations included Rome, Florence, Venice, the Lakes, Amalfi Coast and Tuscany – but we also offer rooms at many lesser known places. Room Service is one of the first companies to recognise the growing trend towards independent travel and was formed specifically to cater to these clients. We

offer a range of affordable yet attractive hotels (too small to be featured by the major tour operators) which provide personal service due to being family run, plus a good standard of accommodation in their category. We personally inspect all hotels and send each client a questionnaire on their return from their holiday. For 1994 we will also offer a small range of self-catering apartments, plus accommodation in beautiful private houses owned by British people living in Italy.'

Hotel holidays: All over Italy

Rosemary & Frances Villas
Time Off, Chester Close,
London SW1X 7BQ
Admin: 071-235 8825
Res: 071-235 8825
Fax: 071-259 6093
ABTA: 58374
ATOL: 2315
AITO
Credit cards: VISA ACCESS

'Rosemary and Frances Villas is a division of Time Off (the city break tour operator) and specialises in the rental of villas and apartments with swimming pools. Our properties are situated in Tuscany, Umbria and the Amalfi coast. Most of our properties have been visited by us and have been chosen for their quality and/or location. We offer privately-owned properties

and though our brochure only shows a small selection of villas and apartments we have a portfolio of over 300 houses. We specialise in "tailormaking" holidays for those who prefer to stay in quieter places – those for whom a private villa with its own pool has more appeal than a hotel in a busy beach resort. Each booking is handled on a personal basis and using our detailed knowledge of Italian villas we take care to make sure our clients book the property that best suits their varied needs.'

Self-catering holidays: Tuscany, Umbria, Venice and the Veneto

Sardatur Holidays
Glen House,
200/208 Tottenham Court Road, London W1P 9LA
Admin: 071-637 0648
Res: 071-637 0281
Fax: 071-580 1535
ATOL: 2593
Credit cards: VISA ACCESS

'Established in 1987, we are the only UK tour operator exclusively featuring Sardinia. We have extensive local knowledge of the island. For the summer we base our tours on a special British Airways flight, direct from Heathrow to Cagliari every Saturday, a service we introduced in 1993. We particularly feature self-catering apartments and villas and always include a self-drive car within the holiday price. We also arrange special interest holidays including walking, horseriding, steam railways, bird watching and golf. We tailor holidays to meet exact requirements and our services can only be booked direct.'

Hotel holidays: Sardinia

Self-catering holidays: Sardinia

Special interest holidays: Horseriding, Walking and trekking

Sherpa Expeditions

131a Heston Road,
Hounslow, Middx TW5 ORD
Admin: 081-569 6627
Res: 081-577 2717
Fax: 081-572 9788
ATOL: 1185
Credit cards: VISA ACCESS

'Sherpa is a company dedicated to walkers and walking holidays – this has been our only activity. We do not offer adventure tours with the odd day's walk thrown in. We have been in operation for over 20 years. We offer a range of walks to suit all tastes and levels of experience. We carry around 2500 people annually. Our destinations in Italy include Tuscany and the Dolomites.'

Special interest holidays: Walking and trekking

Skybus Holidays

24a Earls Court Gardens,
London SW5 0TA
Admin: 071-370 6986
Res: 071-373 6055
Fax: 071-373 6650
ABTA: 4398
ATOL: 2512
Credit cards: VISA ACCESS AMEX

Skybus Holidays offers the Italian Dream programme which includes city breaks to Venice, Florence and Rome as well as resort holidays to the Venice Lido, Sorrento and the Tuscan coast. 'You are free to choose from a selection of charter and scheduled flights and because our specially selected hotels are priced on a nightly basis, you are also free to choose how long you wish to stay at your holiday destination, whether it's just for a few nights at one hotel or a combination of several nights at different cities and resorts.'

Hotel holidays: Tuscany, Naples and surrounding region

Special interest holidays: City breaks

Sovereign

Astral Towers,
Betts Way, Crawley,
West Sussex RH10 2GX
Admin: 0293 599988
Res: 0293 599988
Fax: 0293 588322
ABTA: 68342

ATOL: 230
Credit cards: VISA ACCESS
'Sovereign is part of the Owner's Abroad Group and has been established for 23 years.'
Hotel holidays: Tuscany, Naples and surrounding region
Self-catering holidays: Naples, Sardinia and surrounding region, Lakes, Tuscany, Umbria
Special interest holidays: City breaks

Spes Travel
18 Church Street, London SW1V 2LL
Admin: 071-821 5144
Res: 071-821 5144
Fax: 071-821 6592
ABTA: 56364
ATOL: 263
'Spes Travel has been arranging pilgrimages/holidays for over 30 years. We are a small company which gives us the opportunity to treat clients as individuals and not just as numbers. We arrange trips for about 4000 people each year, many of whom travel each year with us. We specialise in religious holidays, which include many excursions and various itineraries. We take a great deal of trouble to find the right type of accommodation. Each tour is accompanied by a Priest and as the number of participants in each group is about 40 he is able to give each person individual attention, should they so wish. We have had the same courier in Italy for over 15 years, and between the two of them they are able to form the party into a cheerful and stimulating group of friends.'
Special interest holidays: Pilgrimages

Sunsites
Canute Court, Toft Road, Knutsford WA16 0NL
Admin: 0565 625555
Res: 0565 625555
ABTA: 56449
AITO
Credit cards: VISA ACCESS
Sunsites are specialists in self-drive camping and mobile home holidays to Europe and are owned by Eurocamp. 'We have been organising camping holidays for more than 20 years. We offer more than forty sites scattered across four European countries. In Italy our sites are in Tuscany, Venice and the Lakes.'
Special interest holidays: Camping

Sunvil Holidays
7 & 8 Upper Square, Isleworth, Middx TW7 7BJ
Admin: 081-568 4499
Res: 081-568 4499
Fax: 081-568 8330
ABTA: 71398
ATOL: 808

AITO

Credit cards: VISA ACCESS

'Sunvil has been operating for 24 years and is an independently owned specialist company. Our Fly-Drives and Islands programme carries approximately 1000 passengers annually. In Italy we offer holidays to Tuscany, Umbria, the Northern Lakes and Dolomites and Sicily. These are based on flexible fly-drive arrangements. For 1994 we can now include rail travel to Tuscan and Umbrian towns, as well as the main cities of Florence, Venice and Rome. Single and multi-centred holidays can be arranged, with suggested itineraries in the brochure. Alternatively clients can call to discuss a tailor made itinerary. The accommodation has been chosen, wherever possible, as much for its character as its location – the farmhouses in Sicily are a good example. Non-standard holiday durations – a week in a city, or resort and a week's fly-drive, flying in and out of different foreign airports are all possibilities. These holidays are aimed towards the more independently minded traveller – people who would rather gain an insight into the country they are visiting, than lie on a beach for a week or two.'

Hotel holidays: Tuscany, Umbria, Sicily, Lakes, Rome and surrounding region, Venice and the Veneto

Self-catering holidays: Sicily, Tuscany

Swan Hellenic

77 New Oxford Street,

London WC1A 1PP

Admin: 071-831 1515

Res: 071-831 1515

ATOL: 307

Swan Hellenic has been operating cultural cruises for 40 years. 'The 1994 programme comprises 18 different themed cruises around the Mediterranean. Our cruising experience is far more than a relaxing way to travel to some of the more interesting places in the Western world. It's about absorbing atmospheres of both yesteryear and today and breathing life into aspects of history most of us vaguely remember but perhaps never truly understood. Our itineraries are mostly of two weeks' duration but during the summer there are two one-week cruises which can also be linked with adjacent itineraries to form two, three or four week holidays. All our journeys are value for money with no annoying hidden extras, for all main excursions, together with some alternative trips, are included in the fare and there is a no tipping policy on board.'

Special interest holidays: Cruises

Tasting Italy
97 Bravington Road, London W9 3AA
Admin: 081-964 5839
Res: 081-964 5839
Fax: 071-287 2997
'We have been trading for two years, running eight courses a year. We are not part of a larger organisation. We carry approximately 80 people a year. Tasting Italy is a series of one week cookery courses hosted by leading Italian chefs including Valentina Harris and Carla Tomasi. Each course provides the opportunity to develop one's skills in the whole process of Italian culinary arts with special emphasis, not only on cooking, but on choosing and buying fresh produce. The course is designed to give the keen amateur, in a relaxed and informal environment, a basis of confidence on which to build, be inspired and create. It offers the chance to experience the essential role that a good table plays in Italian family life and to appreciate the vast diversity of regional specialities. We stay in beautiful houses and palazzos. The family of the houses are always around, they dine with us and generally make us feel at home. We

have selected three regions – Sicily, Piedmont and Tuscany – each providing different styles of cooking and have timed the courses to take advantage of seasonal specialities and food festivals (sagras). There are plenty of tasting sessions to explore the differences and subtleties of local specialities (olive oils, local cheeses etc) and trips to local markets. An essential part of our courses are the visits, tastings and talks by wine producers which illustrate their passion for winemaking and belief in the increasing quality and stature of Italian wine.'
Special interest holidays: Cooking holidays

The Caravan Club
East Grinstead House,
East Grinstead RH19 1UA
Admin: 0342 326944
Res: 0342 316101
Fax: 0342 327989
Credit cards: VISA ACCESS
'The Caravan Club has 285,000 members in the UK and Ireland. Founded in 1907 by 11 horse-drawn caravan enthusiasts, The Club operates a large private network of sites (currently 202) in the UK and more are planned. The Club's Travel Service was set up more than 20 years ago and now offers a booking service to over 170 continental

161

campsites, as well as a range of inclusive and speciality holidays and a comprehensive holiday insurance which caters specifically for the caravanner. Currently more than 40,000 families travel abroad every year on holidays organised by The Club. We collaborate with three campsites in Italy, one on the shores of Lake Garda and two on or near the northern Adriatic coast near Venice. Members may book as many nights as they wish on these campsites, giving them the freedom of a touring holiday or the choice of a longer stay in one resort. The Club's other services to its members taking foreign holidays include mumerous special offers – many of them exclusive – with all the major ferry operators, holiday insurance with a 24-hour emergency service operating all year, route planning, maps and guides.'

Special interest holidays: Caravans

The Sicilian Experience

6 Palace Street,
London SW1E 5HY
Admin: 071-828 9171
Res: 071-828 9171
Fax: 071-630 5184
ABTA: 0933
ATOL: 2699
Credit cards: VISA ACCESS AMEX

'The Sicilian Experience is a small specialist company which has been trading for 22 years. All areas of Sicily and the Eolian Islands are featured as well as tailor made bookings for the whole of Italy.'

Hotel holidays: Sicily
Self-catering holidays: Sicily

The Travel Club of Upminster

Station Road,
Upminster, Essex RM14 2TT
Admin: 0708 223000
Res: 0708 225000
Fax: 0708 229678
ABTA: 59165
ATOL: 172
AITO
Credit cards: VISA ACCESS

'The Travel Club of Upminster is a family-run company that has been in business since 1936. It is not a club. We sell about 25,000 holidays a year, directly to the public, not through travel agents. We have been taking people to the Italian Lakes since the 1950s and specialise in Lake Orta. In 1993 we introduced our 'Discovery' holidays, aimed at the traveller who wants to discover a little more about the country he or she is visiting. Included under this heading are: The Wine and Gastronomy of the Italian Lakes; The Gardens of the Italian Lakes and Painting in the Italian Lakes. The quality

of our local, English-speaking guides is essential to the success of these holidays. Each of these weeks is based around accommodation at excellent family-run hotels and can easily be extended for an extra week of relaxation. Flights are scheduled services with Alitalia to Milan.'
Hotel holidays: Lakes
Special interest holidays: Garden tours

Thermalia Travel
12 New College Parade,
Finchley Road,
London NW3 5EP
Admin: 071-586 7725
Res: 071 483 1898
Fax: 071-722 7218
ABTA: 005
Credit cards: VISA ACCESS
'We are a fully bonded tour operator offering spa holidays to Italy and Hungary. We have been trading for two years and we sell approximately 500 holidays each year.'
Special interest holidays: Spa holidays

Thomson
Greater London House,
Hampstead Road, London
NW1 7SD
Admin: 071-387 9321
Res: 081-200 8733
ABTA: 5217
ATOL: 2524
Credit cards: VISA ACCESS

Part of the Thomson Travel Group, Thomson Tour Operations has been trading since 1965. It is the UK's largest tour operator carrying over three million holidaymakers per year on air-inclusive packages. In Italy, Thomson feature holidays on the Venetian, Adriatic and Neapolitan Rivieras, the lakes and mountain region, skiing in the winter and city breaks to Rome, Florence and Venice.
Hotel holidays: Adriatic Coast, Naples and surrounding region, Lakes
Self-catering holidays: Adriatic Coast
Special interest holidays: Skiing, City breaks

Timescape Holidays
581 Roman Road,
London E3 5EL
Admin: 081-980 7244
Res: 081-980 7244
Fax: 081-980 7157
ABTA: 83200
Credit cards: VISA ACCESS
'Timescape Holidays has been trading successfully for almost a decade and is a bonded member of ABTA. It is a leading independent operator of value for money coach holidays to Italy. Resorts include Lake Garda and the Lido di Jesolo. Accommodation ranges from self-catering apartments with swimming pools to simple

pensioni and top hotels.'
Special interest holidays:
Coach holidays, Music holidays

Top Deck Travel
131-135 Earls Court Road,
London SW5 9RH
Admin: 071-244 8641
Res: 071-373 4906
Fax: 071-373 6201
ABTA: 59767
AITO
Credit cards: VISA ACCESS
AMEX
'Top Deck Travel is a unique adventure tour operator. Founded in 1973, the original idea was to operate budget tours for the overseas traveller using British double-decker buses. Over the 20 years that Top Deck has been in operation the aims are still very much the same. The fleet of around 50 Deckerhomes in 1989 has gradually been reduced to make way for modern coaches but the Deckerhomes are still the most novel, unique and safe way to travel. Top Deck now operates coach hotel, coach concept style (cabins, fixed site tent villages, chalets etc) holidays, coach camping and the Deckerhomes to all parts of Europe, as far north as the Arctic Circle, as far south as Africa and as far east as Kathmandu. Top Deck also offers tours to Egypt and South America and skiing holidays to Andorra, Austria, Switzerland and France.'
Special interest holidays:
Coach holidays

Traditional Tuscany
108 Westcombe Park Road,
London SE3 7RZ
Admin: 081-305 1380
Res: 081-305 1380
'This is our ninth year as a small independent organisation – very much a family-based affair, both in Italy and here. We carried 140 people last year. Our size allows us to know all our clients personally. We also know all the properties well, visiting at least once every year and keeping in close contact with the owners. Our properties include a castle, traditional villas, farmhouses and cottages, often of historical interest, on country estates set in beautiful surroundings and belonging to old Tuscan families. The owners have maintained their traditions of wine making and farming over generations and are closely involved with the properties. The five estates are in the hills east of Florence or further south towards the Umbrian border. Our brochure explains the characteristics and opportunities of the different regions. We provide a house guide giving more detailed

local information. We can also provide a guide to Italian gardens and to special interest museums. We offer characteristically Italian country holidays. As one owner says "Immersi in una vita antica . . . in Toscana.'
Self-catering holidays: Tuscany

Travel for the Arts
117 Regent's Park Road,
London NW1 8UR
Admin: 071-483 4466
Res: 071-483 4466
Fax: 071-586 0639
ABTA: 98916
ATOL: 2970
Credit cards: VISA ACCESS
'Travel for the Arts is a division of Blair Travel & Leisure which has been trading since 1988. We are a small specialist company providing holidays for music lovers. There are different categories: escorted tours for small groups of not more than 30 people accompanied by a tour manager; tours run throughout the opera season to many of Italy's great opera houses. The carefully planned itineraries include scheduled air travel, comfortable hotel accomodation, tickets for at least one opera, ballet or concert performance, a guided sightseeing programme covering the cultural highlights and any particular places of musical interest; escorted tours to

summer festivals throughout Italy; and a la carte holidays for the independent traveller.'
Special interest holidays: Music holidays

Tuscany – from Cottages to Castles
Tuscany House,
351 Tonbridge Road,
Maidstone, Kent ME16 8NH
Admin: 0622 726883
Res: 0622 726883
Fax: 0622 729835
ATOL: 3037
Credit cards: VISA ACCESS
'Tuscany – from Cottages to Castles has been established since 1982. We are currently carrying approximately 8000 passengers a year. We offer self-catering holidays in Tuscany and Umbria. Our sales team have visited all of our properties and are able to advise and guide our customers in choosing the right apartment or villa. Flights, car hire, ferry or Motorail can also be arranged.'
Self-catering holidays: Tuscany, Umbria

Tuscany Now
274-276 Seven Sisters Road,
London N4
Admin: 071-272 5469
Res: 071-272 5469
Fax: 071-272 6184
'Tuscany Now is an owner-managed company that began trading in 1989 with the aim

of introducing to the independent traveller what we believe to be the most beautiful and most loved area in Europe, Tuscany. Using over 20 years of experience of living in Tuscany and other areas in Italy, and of running our own self-catering villa in the Valdarno region just outside Florence, we have spent a great deal of time personally searching for the perfect holiday situation. We specialise in property in Tuscany and Umbria. Our brochure consists of a wide collection of carefully selected private villas, farmhouses, apartments and hotels with pools and tennis courts. In 1993 we carried 4000 people to Tuscany. Of particular interest is the fact that we own some of our properties and we also deal directly with the owners thus enabling the prices to be affordable to all. By building a good relationship with the owners we are able to give our clients a better service. Each and every property has been inspected by ourselves – again this enables us to assure our clients of our vast knowledge of the properties, the surrounding towns and shops, information on historic places of interest, where to purchase good Chianti wine at prices considerably lower than market prices, or information on ballooning trips over Siena! Our hotel range covers all areas of Italy.'
Self-catering holidays: Tuscany, Umbria

Vacanze in Italia
Bignor, Pulborough,
West Sussex RH20 1QD
Admin: 07987 461
Res: 07987 426
Fax: 07987 343
ATOL: 2433
AITO
Credit cards: VISA ACCESS
'Vacanze in Italia forms part of the Vere Leisure Group which owns English Country Cottages. We have just celebrated 10 years of providing holiday accommodation in many of the most beautiful regions of Italy. In our 1994 brochure we present a selection of some 300 properties. The emphasis is on houses set in the classical landscapes of Tuscany and Umbria. We also continue to feature Asti, the Marches and the Tuscan coast. We also offer properties in Florence and Rome.'
Self-catering holidays: Tuscany, Umbria, Rome and surrounding region

Venetian Apartments
38 Palmerston Road,
London SW14 7PZ
Admin: 081-878 1130
Res: 081-878 1130
Fax: 081-878 0982

'Venetian Apartments offers a range of central apartments from simple studios to apartments in luxury palazzo properties in Venice, Rome and Florence. It is very much a personalised service where great care is taken to match suitable properties to the right clients. The apartments are described clearly and honestly, and if a particular property is not for you we'll find something else. Flights are co-ordinated through an ABTA travel agency to ensure a smooth and trouble free trip. Ann-Marie Doyle who runs Venetian Apartments, knows each property and owner personally, and is able to answer any queries about the property or about the holiday in general.'
Self-catering holidays: Venice and the Veneto

Venice Simplon-Orient Express
Sea Containers House,
20 Upper Ground,
London SE1 9PF
Admin: 071-928 6000
Res: 071-928 6000
Fax: 071-620 1210
ATOL: 3141
Credit cards: VISA ACCESS AMEX DINERS
Luxury train service that offers an elegant passage from Victoria station in London to Santa Lucia station in Venice.

Special interest holidays: Train holidays

Venue Holidays
21 Christchurch Road,
Ashford TN23 1XD
Admin: 0233 642505
Res: 0233 629950
Fax: 0233 634494
Credit cards: VISA ACCESS
'We are an independent self-drive tour operator with two resorts in Italy. Venue is a family run business and 1994 will be our 10th season of operation. We market our holidays in the UK, Germany, Holland and Denmark and we carry about 2000 passengers each year. Our two areas of operation in Italy are Punta Sabbioni on the Venetian Riviera and Figline, just south of Florence. Our aim is to offer a traditional and economic family holiday with the possibility of some classic sight-seeing.'
Special interest holidays: Camping

Veronica Tomasso Cotgrove
10 St Mary's Crescent,
Regent's Park,
London NW1 7TS
Admin: 071-267 2423
Res: 071-267 2423
Fax: 071-267 4759
'Veronica Tomasso Cotgrove runs her own organisation renting and selling hand-picked properties in Tuscany,

Umbria and Venice. She formed her own company in 1986. Veronica knows all the properties personally and the Italian owners themselves are amongst her dearest friends with whom she has a happy business association. She can therefore pass on personal recommendations to her clients, having stayed in and constantly visited all the properties.'
Self-catering holidays: Tuscany, Umbria

Verrocchio Arts Centre
41 Norland Square,
London W11 4PZ
Admin: 071-727 3313
Res: 071-727 3313
'The Verrocchio Arts Centre has been holding residential fortnightly courses in painting and sculpture from June to September since 1984 in a converted granary on the edge of the hilltop village of Casole d'Elsa in the heart of rural Tuscany within sight of San Gimignano and half an hour's drive from Siena. The centre, owned and run by sculptor Nigel Konstam and his wife Janet, provides daily tuition, good food, pleasant simple accommodation and a convivial atmosphere for 20 guests. There are roomy studios, a leafy terrace, a small indoor swimming pool, plus a separate kitchen for those who wish to self-cater.'

Special interest holidays: Painting & drawing holidays

Villa Fillinelle
112 Kingsley Park Terrace,
Northampton NN2 7HJ
Admin: 0604 720242
Res: 0604 720242
Fax: 0604 710652
'We are Travel World Business Events, a division of Business Travel World which has been trading for eight years. We are the UK agent for Villa Fillinelle and have been marketing this product in the UK for three years. Villa Fillinelle is a brochure covering the rental of villas and apartments in the Tuscany area of Italy only. Our brochure is ideal for the independent traveller wishing to make his own travel arrangements, although we can provide this service if he so wishes.'
Self-catering holidays: Tuscany

Villas Argentario
Island House, Chiswick Mall,
London W4 2PS
Admin: 081-994 2956
Res: 081-994 2956
Fax: 081-747 8343
'We are an unlimited partnership of husband and wife with many years' experience of living in Italy, offering a service to ensure that our clients get the sort of holiday they want. We have houses

(two of them our own) and apartments to rent in unspoilt countryside with uncrowded beaches. Monte Argentario is almost an island, joined by natural and manmade causeways to the mainland. Development is very restricted. It is one of the wildest parts of the Mediterranean coast. Our tenants write of "perfect tranquility", "incredibly beautiful views" and "lovely beaches". The summer residents are mostly Italian. Our rentals are not cheap, reflecting high property prices because of the block on development, the beauty of the country and the closeness of the beaches, all under 10 minutes away.'
Self-catering holidays: Tuscany

Waymark Holidays
44 Windsor Road,
Slough SL1 2EJ
Admin: 0753 516477
Res: 0753 516477
Fax: 0753 517016
ATOL: 624
Credit cards: VISA
'We are celebrating 20 years as a tour operator. We have always specialised in walking holidays, and although we have expanded our operation into many different countries, we still prefer to concentrate our attentions on the activity we know best – walking. We are a small team, knowledgeable and keen on walking,

and can talk about our holidays from first-hand experience. Walks are graded from one to five. Four hours of walking is involved at grade one, eight hours for grade five. Our parties normally consist of a maximum of 16 people, but there are fewer on tours and at some centres.'
Special interest holidays: Walking and trekking

Winterski/Vita Holidays
31 Old Steine,
Brighton BN1 1EL
Admin: 0273 626242
Res: 0273 626242
Fax: 0273 620222
ABTA: 741
ATOL: 2504
Credit cards: VISA ACCESS
'We are a small company, established in 1983. Our company specialises in Italy, concentrating mainly in the areas of Lombardia and Trentino. We have developed our experience and knowledge of the area to offer a programme including skiing, opera and walking holidays. Specialising in a limited number of resorts means our staff can offer much more to their clients. All staff have first-hand experience of the resort they promote and can offer that much more information.'
Special interest holidays: Skiing, Music holidays, Walking and trekking